Comments on other *Amazing Stories* from readers & reviewers

*"Tightly written volumes filled with lots of wit and humour
about famous and infamous Canadians."*
Eric Shackleton, *The Globe and Mail*

*"The heightened sense of drama and intrigue, combined with a
good dose of human interest is what sets* Amazing Stories *apart."*
Pamela Klaffke, *Calgary Herald*

*"This is popular history as it should be... For this price,
buy two and give one to a friend."*
Terry Cook, a reader from Ottawa, on **Rebel Women**

*"Glasner creates the moment of the explosion itself in
graphic detail...she builds detail upon gruesome detail
to create a convincingly authentic picture."*
Peggy McKinnon, *The Sunday Herald*, on **The Halifax Explosion**

*"It was wonderful...I found I could not put it down.
I was sorry when it was completed."*
Dorothy F. from Manitoba on **Marie-Anne Lagimodière**

*"Stories are rich in description, and bristle
with a clever, stylish realness."*
Mark Weber, *Central Alberta Advisor*, on **Ghost Town Stories II**

*"A compelling read. Bertin...has selected only the most intriguing
tales, which she narrates with a wealth of detail."*
Joyce Glasner, *New Brunswick Reader*, on **Strange Events**

*"The resulting book is one readers will want to share
with all the women in their lives."*
Lynn Martel, *Rocky Mountain Outlook*, on **Women Explorers**

THE MYSTERY
OF THE OAK
ISLAND TREASURE

THE MYSTERY OF THE OAK ISLAND TREASURE

Two Hundred Years
of Hope and Despair

by Mark Reynolds

James Lorimer & Company Ltd., Publishers
Toronto

James Lorimer & Company Ltd., Publishers acknowledges the support of the Ontario Arts Council. We acknowledge the financial support of the Government of Canada through the Canada Book Fund for our publishing activities. We acknowledge the support of the Canada Council for the Arts, which last year invested $24.3 million in writing and publishing through-out Canada. We acknowledge the support of the Government of Ontario through the Ontario Media Development Corporation's Ontario Book Initiative.

ONTARIO ARTS COUNCIL
CONSEIL DES ARTS DE L'ONTARIO

Canada Council
for the Arts

Library and Archives Canada Cataloguing in Publication

Reynolds, Mark
The mystery of the Oak Island treasure : two hundred years of hope and despair / Mark Reynolds. -- Rev. ed.

(Amazing stories)
Includes bibliographical references.
ISBN 978-1-55277-414-4

1. Oak Island Treasure Site (N.S.)--History. 2. Treasure troves--Nova Scotia--Oak Island (Lunenburg)--History. I. Title. II. Series: Amazing stories (Toronto, Ont.)

FC2345.O23R49 2009   971.6'23   C2009-902244-3

James Lorimer & Company Ltd., Publishers
317 Adelaide Street West, Suite 1002
Toronto, ON, Canada
M5V 1P9
www.lorimer.ca

Printed in Canada

For Amynah, my mysterious treasure.

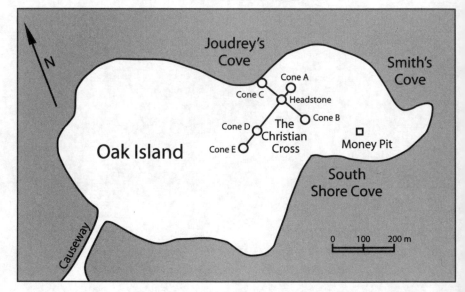

Map of Oak Island, Nova Scotia

Contents

Prologue

Answers. All Dan Blankenship wanted were answers, and the small television screen in front of him might, after so many years of searching, reveal them.

By August of 1971, Blankenship had already been pitting his wits and energies against the mystery of Oak Island for five years. Digging, diving, digging some more, trying to solve a mystery that had already taken six lives on this wooded island in Mahone Bay, Nova Scotia.

Some months before, the drilling efforts in the shaft Blankenship considered most promising — called Borehole 10X — had broken into an underground cavern. Constantly flooded by the waters of Mahone Bay, it was too dangerous to descend into the pit, but intriguing items had come up with the drill — wood and pieces of metal. This was some of the first tangible evidence of treasure in over 100 years of searching on the island.

Today, Blankenship's television screen was hooked up to a remote control underwater camera. It was slowly making its way deeper into the murk of Borehole 10X, where Blankenship believed pirate treasure, or something even more valuable, had been buried centuries before.

At first, there was nothing but dark, salt water and mud

masking the details of the walls of the pit. Deeper went the camera — 60 metres, then 70 metres. Finally something was on screen — a piece of wood. Maybe a pickaxe handle? And just beyond, a chest? And beside it another ... and another. Was this the evidence he had been looking for? If so, it conclusively proved that the search was not in vain, and that the curse that supposedly guarded the treasure was a myth. But then something else came on the flickering screen, floating in the water. A disembodied hand, severed at the wrist. And slumped over by the chamber wall, a body.

Chapter 1
Discovery

aniel McGinnis could barely contain his excitement as he led his friends John Smith and Anthony Vaughan through the wooded shade of Oak Island in the early summer of 1795. The three teenagers had grown up in the nearby town of Chester, 6 kilometres away on the shores of Mahone Bay, Nova Scotia.

Daniel had been exploring the island just the day before. Now his two friends followed him through the trees of the near empty island to a small clearing on the southeastern end. When they arrived in the clearing they could see an oak tree, one of the many from which the island took its name. Hanging from a forked branch was an old tackle block from a ship.

The clearing was man-made. The three young men could see numerous tree stumps and remnants of trees cut some years before. But who had cut them? Daniel's father and another farmer were the only men who owned land on the island, and neither had been there long enough to have done this kind of work. In addition, the logs that one would have expected from natural tree-falls were nowhere to be seen.

Tree stumps were not what interested the boys right then. The cause of Daniel's excitement was a depression in the ground under the dangling ship's tackle. Though it was grown over with vegetation, the boys could tell that whatever had caused this irregularity was not natural. Daniel and his companions knew right away that whatever they had found, it had to be important.

Though it is only one of over 300 islands in Mahone Bay, Oak Island was a source of speculation and fear in the nearby town of Chester. Called, at various times, Gloucester Island and Smith's Island, Oak Island got its name by being the only island of the hundreds dotting the bay to have red oaks growing on it. Situated roughly 150 metres from the western shore of the bay, the island is about 1.5 kilometres long and 1 kilometre wide. Well away from the normal shipping lanes, it is hidden from view of the main body of water by larger islands. No higher than 10 metres at any point, the island is largely swamp in its south central area.

Oak Island was part of a large grant of land the British colonial authorities initially called Shoreham, which later became Chester. The area around the island was settled by colonists from New England. At the time of Daniel's discovery, only some of the 32 four-acre lots on the island had been purchased. Some were under cultivation by Samuel Ball, a freed slave from South Carolina, and the rest were owned by Daniel McGinnis Sr. Chester, roughly 70 kilometres southwest of Halifax, had been settled since 1759. In the 36 years before young Daniel made his discovery, locals had traded stories about Oak Island.

It was an ominous place. Strange lights had been seen in years past. Men were seen working in the light of bonfires. Legend had it that when two brave locals went to the island one year to find out about these men, the pair disappeared, never to be seen again. Whoever these men were, they obviously didn't want to be observed. But even those most wary about prying into the mysteries of the island couldn't help but consider that maybe, just maybe, the island could be hiding treasure. Pirate treasure.

In the heyday of the pirates, there was almost no settlement on Nova Scotia's South Shore. The numerous inlets, harbours, and bays made ideal hiding places for buccaneers looking to avoid the navies of Britain, France, and Spain. Best of all was Mahone Bay, its islands providing a watery maze for concealment.

And if it were pirate treasure hidden out there, why not the legendary treasure of Captain William Kidd? That horde, captured from uncounted East Indian merchant vessels, would be enough to make whoever found it rich beyond their wildest dreams.

The most notorious pirate of his day, the Scots-born Kidd was a man who enjoyed friends in high places. After winning the favour of the British as a privateer — basically a pirate with a government commission — Kidd found his way to New York. In the late 1600s, New York was a friendly port for men of his profession. Using his political connections, Kidd managed to obtain a commission from King William in 1696 to hunt pirates and attack enemy commerce in the Indian Ocean.

Had Kidd contented himself with staying within the bounds of his commissions, he never would have gained the notoriety that he did. However, he quickly decided his fortune lay in turning buccaneer himself. Over the next few years he looted and robbed on the high seas, taking merchant ships of every nationality — including those of Britain's allies.

The life of a pirate, or even a more legitimate privateer, was not an easy one. Long months at sea, with a crew that was generally loyal only to themselves and the lure of gold, required nerves of steel and an iron fist of discipline. There were few friendly ports for supplies, and maintenance often needed to be carried out on remote islands where the natives could be more dangerous than enemy ships.

Many of Kidd's crew were inexperienced mariners, although it was often possible to attract good men from the ports, especially those who wanted to escape the hard life of the Royal Navy, which rarely allowed for the possibility of plunder.

As Kidd's exploits illustrate, taking enemy merchant vessels was often the easiest part of the job. It was rarely like the epic battles depicted in Hollywood movies — merchant vessels would usually flee before they would fight and, when caught, rarely had the weaponry to defend themselves. Even when they did, sailors were unlikely to risk their lives to protect the cargo of their employers. Sometimes captains would even pay a fee to attackers in order to keep their ships and cargo, making piracy an exercise in taxation more than swordplay.

Kidd's ship, the *Adventure Galley*, left England in April of 1696. He and his crew headed to New York to take on more men and supplies, and here Kidd was able to see his wife once more before his voyage. His crew was largely made up of landless, desperate, or simply adventurous young men, rough and ready for battle. Upon reaching the Indian Ocean after a long, hard voyage, during which Kidd lost dozens of men to disease, Kidd almost immediately abandoned his commission. He attacked and took several small merchant vessels, but none were very valuable. Finally, on January 8, 1698, Kidd spotted and took the *Quedah Merchant*, an Indian vessel loaded with cloth, iron, opium, and other valuable goods. The crew of the *Quedah Merchant* surrendered to Kidd without a fight.

He returned to New York in 1699, with a crew of only 20 — many of his men had left him to join other ships when the voyage was over, others had died. He had abandoned the

Adventure Galley in favour of the *Quedah Merchant*, which he took as far as Barbados before acquiring yet another ship. News of his adventures in the East had preceded him. Unfortunately for him, the political tide had turned against piracy. His disruption of trade had made him powerful enemies in the East Indian colonies. A warrant was issued for his arrest, and he was promptly thrown in jail by the governor of New York — a man who had been an investor in Kidd's voyage.

Stories flew about the wealth Kidd had accumulated. Some said it was worth as much as £500,000, an incredible sum in those days. The governor sent out ships to the Caribbean — Kidd's former hideout, where he had stopped on his return to North America — to search for the booty. They returned empty.

Kidd was sent to London for trial on charges of murder and piracy. He was found guilty on all counts, and sentenced to be hanged. Desperate, he tried one last gambit to escape death. He offered to buy his life in exchange for divulging the location of his horde. The offer was rejected, and Kidd was hanged on May 23, 1701. His body was wrapped in chains and left dangling next to the Thames, where it would serve as a warning to all who saw it.

The legend of Kidd's treasure lived on, especially in the colonies where it was a source of fevered speculation up and down the eastern seaboard. One story had it that sometime in the 1700s, an old man, lying on his deathbed, claimed to have been a crewmember of the notorious pirate. He said that he had helped Kidd bury his treasure somewhere on an island east of Boston. Although hundreds searched, no treasure was ever found.

The old folk of Mahone Bay were all transplanted New Englanders, and they would have known the story of the old man and others like it. They also would have known the legends of how pirates ensured their treasure would not be found by others.

Landing on a moonlit beach on some unmapped isle, a boatload of pirates would row ashore, shovels in hand. Finding an appropriate spot, they would dig, drinking and carousing next to a roaring bonfire as they did so. As their chest of treasure was lowered into the ground, the captain would ask for one man to volunteer to guard the booty until his mates could return. Of course, all would volunteer. There was no honour among thieves — the lucky man to get this assignment could easily have the whole treasure to himself. One man would shout louder than the others for the job, and the captain would choose him. As the night wore on the men would sing sea chanties and outdo one another with tales of the lavish lives they would lead with the booty in the ground below them, getting more and more drunk. Finally, as dawn drew near and the men were too inebriated to stand straight, the captain would approach the volunteer guard. Catching him by surprise, the captain would bash him over the head with a cudgel, and then order his crew to throw him into the pit, to be buried alive. His ghost would stand sentry for eternity.

No sensible man, the old folk of Chester would mutter, would poke around a place like Oak Island. However, Daniel McGinnis and his friends were in no mood to be sensible. Knowing that just below them might lay wealth beyond imagining, they could barely contain themselves.

The first order of business was to investigate the ship's tackle. Upon climbing the tree to where it hung, they discovered it was held in place by a wooden peg. They managed to get the tackle loose, but in their hurry dropped it. It shattered on the ground. The loss of this important clue was not seen as a big deal at the time. There was so much evidence of men's work here, one more item hardly mattered. For instance, from the clearing were the remains of an old road, which led to the western portion of the island. On the island's shore they discovered a ringbolt set in a rock, perhaps to moor a small boat. And of course, there was the depression in the ground. This was shortly to become known as the Money Pit. It was a circular hole, four metres in diameter, dipping about 30 centimetres below the surrounding soil. And it was soon much lower. The three young men, used to hard labour in what were still pioneer days on Canada's East Coast, were certain that all that stood between them and a life of leisure was a few hours of digging.

The Money Pit soon showed itself to be a much more complicated structure than they thought. After digging only half a metre, the boys encountered a layer of flagstones,

Present-day Oak Island, with South Shore Cove in the background. The Money Pit can be seen to the right of the fenced-in enclosure. The mounds in the background are the result of Robert Dunfield's excavations in 1966–1967.

which were not like the stone found on the island. These were removed, and the digging continued.

The warmth of the early summer day, cut by the shade of the trees, would have made the effort seem like a lark to the boys. The digging was not hard anyway. The pit was evidently an old shaft that had been filled in. Although the walls were hard-packed clay, the dirt within was loose and easy to remove. At a depth of three metres, the boys' efforts paid off with the sound of their shovel blades hitting wood. This must be it! Treasure chests, filled with doubloons! Gemstones, and all the riches of the Orient!

Their elation swiftly turned to disappointment and curiosity. The wood turned out to be a platform of oak logs embedded in the sides of the shaft. It was not treasure, but it was almost as good. This was proof that someone, likely the same someone who had created the clearing, had buried something. The boys dug further, removing the logs. There was a cavity underneath, caused by the settling of the earth. They dug further, and still further. Finally, at a depth of eight metres, they admitted that they would get no further without the aid of others. They placed wooden stakes around the pit and covered it with brush, fully expecting to return soon.

Daniel, John, and Anthony returned to Chester with tales of what they had found, but it was to no avail. Perhaps the townsfolk discounted their story as the romantic fantasy of youth, the games young men play at in the summer months. Chester was a working town — there was land to be tilled, fish to be caught. No one wanted to waste their time poking around in the dirt on a fool's errand.

The trio was not dissuaded. So sure were they that they had found something important that the eldest of the three, John Smith, purchased Lot 18, which included the Pit. Over the years, he would go on to buy more Oak Island lots until he was the sole owner of the eastern end of the island. Daniel McGinnis also settled on the island, and Anthony Vaughan began farming on the western shore, not far away.

Discovery

The summer of 1795 turned to autumn, then winter. In all, seven years would pass before another attempt was made to find the treasure.

Chapter 2
The Booby Trap

n the summer of 1803, a small sailing vessel left the town of Onslow, on the Bay of Fundy. Loaded with digging equipment, it was meant to be embarking on a voyage of discovery. Moving gracefully before the wind, it made the roundabout voyage down the shores of Fundy, past Yarmouth and the southernmost tip of Nova Scotia where it juts into the Atlantic. Turning northeast it followed the coast until it reached the island-strewn waters of Mahone Bay, a 350-kilometre voyage in all.

The boat was met at Oak Island by the three discoverers of the Money Pit and their families. For years they had been waiting anxiously for this moment, spending the last winter in agonizing anticipation of the wealth that would be theirs. No more would the women need to scrub their own floors or mend old dresses by candlelight. No more would the men have to patch their leaky old boats. They could fill their wardrobes with all the best clothes from England and the United States, and hold their heads high amongst the city folk when they sailed into Halifax in their fine new sloops.

It had been a hard seven years since the summer of 1795. With the three men living on or near the island, they were able to keep an eye on their treasure while they searched for a financial backer for another attempt on the Pit. The community of Chester was not wealthy enough to provide the means to hire the men and buy the equipment that would be required to dig further. It is also possible the three wanted to limit local involvement, in order to better protect their treasure.

In 1802, they found the man they were looking for. According to one version of the story, John Smith's wife became pregnant. Believing Oak Island to be cursed, she refused to have her baby on the family farm. They travelled to Truro, where the child was delivered by Dr. Simeon Lynd. John revealed the secret of the Pit to the doctor, telling him about the strange structure of the shaft and the history of the island. Intrigued, Lynd returned to Chester with the Smiths to inspect the island. He went away convinced that there was great wealth to be found in the soil of Oak Island. He formed the Onslow Company and appointed Colonel Robert Archibald, a surveyor and justice of the peace, as director of operations.

When the men of the Onslow Company arrived at

the Pit, they discovered that it had collapsed in on itself. However, when they cleared the debris and brush from the area, they found the stakes McGinnis and his friends had driven into the ground years before, which indicated that no one else had dug into the hole.

As the Onslow Company workers probed ever deeper into the Pit, the mystery only deepened. As McGinnis, Vaughan, and Smith had done years ago, the men set to work with shovels. Hearts leapt with excitement at the sound of metal hitting wood. They shovelled at a frantic pace, only to uncover another platform of oak logs. This obstacle cleared, digging commenced again. Three metres farther down, a layer of charcoal was encountered and removed. Another three metres into the shaft was a layer of putty.

There was still no sign of treasure, but the consistency of the layers gave hope to the partners. Whoever had made the Money Pit had gone to great lengths to hide their treasure, indicating that it was valuable indeed. The Pit was already 27 metres deep.

Finally, the shovel of one of the men hit a stone. More dirt was cleared away in order to remove this newest obstacle, but it soon became apparent that this was no ordinary stone. The gray rock, not a type found around Mahone Bay, was 35 centimetres by 60 centimetres, and marked on one side with unusual characters. The inscription on the stone was not in any language or using any alphabet that the men on the island could decipher. Was it a code? Some sort of ancient artifact? A key of some sort to the mystery? ·

The stone became the first proof that the Money Pit held something more mysterious than Kidd's doubloons. Some among the partners may already have been realizing that no pirate would have had the means or the discipline to dig so deep to hide a treasure for which they planned to return.

The men didn't concern themselves too much with the rock at first. They set about digging again — they were close now, they knew it. But as they dug, something strange started to happen. Water began seeping into the Pit. Soon it was entering the Pit at a rate that forced them to remove two buckets of water for every one of soil. Nonetheless, they continued, and as night fell they began to pack up. They probed the bottom of the Pit with rods, poking into the mucky earth. Through the dirt, the rods hit a hard surface of some sort that covered the entire diameter of the shaft at a depth of about 30 metres. They retired for the night, certain that the next day they would be millionaires. What a shock it must have been the next day when they returned to the Money Pit to claim their reward. The shaft was filled with seawater from a depth of 11 metres, roughly the level of Mahone Bay.

Somehow, whoever had constructed the Money Pit had set a trap — dig to a certain depth, and flood tunnels connected to the bay would fill the tunnel with water. Perhaps in removing the stone the men of the Onslow Company had somehow triggered the mechanism that would protect the secret of the Pit.

At this point, unaware of the flood tunnels, the men believed the flooding to be a result of natural seepage, and set about removing the water. The workers attacked the Pit with buckets, bailing out the seawater as quickly as they could. It was to no avail. The level of the water remained the same, fluctuating only with the tides around the island.

This was a problem beyond the immediate resources of the Onslow Company. They were forced to halt operations for the next few months, and go back to work on their farms for the summer.

In the fall, the company contracted the services of a Mr. Mosher from Hants County, who they paid £80 to set up a pump to remove the water. That autumn the pump was sent to the bottom of the shaft, but burst without lowering the water level at all.

Colonel Archibald decided to give up for the winter, and spent the cold months of early 1804 plotting his next attempt on the Pit. Perhaps his military background gave him the idea of a flanking assault. Rather than continue wasting money and time trying to drain the water, Archibald decided to go around it.

Picking a spot several metres away from the Money Pit, Archibald directed his workers to start digging anew. They sunk a new shaft, almost 35 metres deep, parallel to the original. They then began to dig a connecting tunnel. With luck, they would be able to enter the Money Pit below the level of the hard surface they had felt the previous year before the Pit had flooded. They would then be able to recover the treasure from beneath the water.

It was not to be. As they neared the outer walls of the old shaft, water began to seep in. Undaunted, they kept digging, pushing nearer to their goal. Suddenly, the walls collapsed. Thousands of gallons of seawater rushed into the tunnel. Shouting and panicking, the men fled, barely escaping the second shaft alive. The water continued pouring in, and soon the second shaft was filled with water to the same level as the Money Pit.

Though no one was harmed, this represented a disaster for the Onslow Company. There were no more funds to make another attempt on the Pit, and the volume of water pouring in from the sea was beyond the capabilities of the technology of the day.

The dreams of John Smith, Daniel McGinnis, and Anthony Vaughan were drowned in that rush of water. For 10 years they had been certain that, should they get to the bottom of the Pit, they would never have to worry about money again. When news of this failure spread, there would be no chance others would invest. Perhaps the island was cursed after all.

Perhaps, but the lure of Oak Island could not be resisted forever. Another attempt would be made on the island, but it would be 45 years before the next company was formed to crack the mystery.

Chapter 3
The Flood Tunnel

here was nothing for the three men to do but return to their farms and put their boyhood dreams of pirate booty behind them. Families needed to be fed, crops tended to, livestock cared for.

John Smith had no gold, but he did have the stone slab the diggers had uncovered before the Pit had flooded. No one in the Onslow Company could make sense of the strange markings on the stone. It may have been some sort of code, or perhaps an inscription in a foreign alphabet, but in Nova Scotia in the early 19th century there was no one to decipher it.

With all the years and effort Smith had sunk into the Money Pit, he was not going to toss aside the only item his effort had yielded so far. The strange stone would serve as an interesting centrepiece for his new fireplace, something for visitors to speculate about for years to come.

And there were plenty of visitors after the failed attempt of the Onslow Company. Word travelled fast in the small province, and there seemed little point in keeping the Pit a secret anymore. Hundreds of the curious made the short trip to the island. They could look at the remains of the two shafts and maybe stop in for tea at Smith's house, where he would tell them the legends of the island and of Captain Kidd.

Perhaps because he felt it was a danger to his young children, or perhaps because he didn't want to see evidence of his failure, Smith filled in the two shafts over the next few years. He never forgot about them, not even in his old age. Seeing the inscribed stone every day was a tantalizing mystery for him. What could it mean? What lay in the Pit below? When he was in his 70s, he would get another chance to find out.

By 1849, Nova Scotia was becoming a prosperous place. Halifax, not far from Chester, was a major shipping port celebrating its centenary and growing importance in British North America. Work had begun on the Shubenacadie Canal. Then the largest construction project in the British Empire, the canal was designed to connect the colonial capital to the Bay of Fundy, over 100 kilometres away. Steam power was becoming more common, and some visionaries were talking about bringing the locomotive to the province.

With modern-day ingenuity and the right can-do attitude, many figured a mere hole in the ground should be no problem. Thus the Truro Company was formed by a group of Nova Scotia businessmen, including John Gammell, Jotham McCully, and James Pitblado, a mining engineer. The new company spoke with Anthony Vaughan and John Smith to determine the location of the old pits. It doesn't seem that they listened to the warnings that the Pit was a trickier prospect than they thought.

The Truro Company attacked the Pit head-on, as the Onslow Company and McGinnis, Smith, and Vaughan had done before them. Perhaps it was their confidence that led them to disregard the fact that both tunnels had flooded, or perhaps they believed it had been a fluke of some sort. Whatever the reason, the men dug straight down, reaching nearly the same depth that the Onslow Company had before they were thwarted. It being a Saturday night, they stopped for the evening, congratulating each other on their hard work.

The next day, they were confronted with a pit full of seawater. The curse of the island had struck overnight, and now they were back where their predecessors had left off four decades before. History having taught them nothing, they set about bailing the pit, with no success. They were not without other ideas, however. If the treasure could not be recovered by the work of men, then perhaps, they thought, it could be extracted by mechanical means.

Under Pitblado and McCully's direction, the workers of the Truro Company constructed a wooden platform inside the shaft, just above the water level. This would be the base for a drilling device called a pod auger.

A pod auger was used in prospecting for coal. Mining companies could drill into the earth and bring up core samples to determine if there was anything of value below. Pitblado decided to use the auger to discover what was beneath the floor of the Money Pit, and to possibly bring up some samples of Kidd's gold.

With high hopes, the men set to work. The auger was sent down into the murky waters, finally hitting the hard barrier the Onslow Company had probed just before the shaft flooded in 1803, at a depth of 27 metres. Interestingly, the samples sent up by the auger indicated that this barrier was made of spruce wood, meaning that it was, again, something placed there by the hand of man.

Just below the spruce platform the auger again hit wood, this time oak. Then came the sound that the men had been waiting weeks to hear. Just after passing through the oak obstruction — the top of a chest? — the auger began ringing with the sound of metal on metal. Ten centimeters, twenty, thirty — fifty centimetres in all! If this was gold, there was surely enough there to make everyone rich!

The auger continued its downward journey. After passing through the small pieces of metal it hit oak again; this was thought to be the bottom of the chest. Soon after, it hit metal

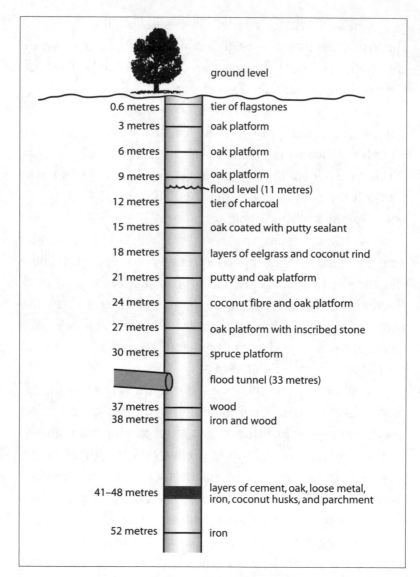

	ground level
0.6 metres	tier of flagstones
3 metres	oak platform
6 metres	oak platform
9 metres	oak platform
	flood level (11 metres)
12 metres	tier of charcoal
15 metres	oak coated with putty sealant
18 metres	layers of eelgrass and coconut rind
21 metres	putty and oak platform
24 metres	coconut fibre and oak platform
27 metres	oak platform with inscribed stone
30 metres	spruce platform
	flood tunnel (33 metres)
37 metres	wood
38 metres	iron and wood
41–48 metres	layers of cement, oak, loose metal, iron, coconut husks, and parchment
52 metres	iron

Diagram of the Money Pit

again, indicating that chests were stacked, one on top of another. The auger sunk another 50 centimetres through the metal, each clink and rattle gleefully noted by the men above. Again the auger passed through oak, then spruce, then into clay. The treasure had been located, over 30 metres below the surface of the island!

In all, the company drilled five holes into the bottom of the Pit. The auger brought up wood shavings and clay; it did not bring up any gold coins. The only man-made objects that came up were some small chain links made of gold, the sort that might decorate a military uniform. The auger was not able to bring up any larger pieces of metal.

It was Pitblado's responsibility to sift through the muck and debris brought up by the auger, preserving it all for later examination. During the drilling of the third hole, Gammell noticed Pitblado off by himself, examining something small in his hand. Not realizing he was being observed, the engineer pocketed the item. Suspicious, Gammell approached Pitblado and asked him to show him what he had found. Pitblado refused, but told Gammell he would show the item at the next meeting of the Truro Company directors. Satisfied, the trusting Gammell did not pursue the matter further.

Pitblado did not attend the next meeting of the directors, nor any other afterwards. He left the island that night and never returned. Whatever he found, it was significant enough to pique the interest of Charles Archibald, manager of the Acadian Ironworks in Londonderry, Nova Scotia. Pitblado must have shared his discovery with the businessman. After meeting with Pitblado, Archibald attempted to buy the portion of Oak Island that contained the Money Pit. He failed in this, and Pitblado disappeared. No one ever found out what he had removed from the auger that day, and no one knows what became of him.

Not discouraged by the defection of their colleague, Gammell, McCully, and the rest of the Truro Company pressed on. In the spring of 1850, they decided to again follow the lead of the Onslow Company, and dig a parallel shaft to the original Money Pit. As with the attempt 45 years earlier, they managed to dig down more than 30 metres without encountering water. Once they began to tunnel towards the Money Pit, however, water again burst into the new shaft, rapidly filling it.

It was only now that the men of the Truro Company began to realize that the Money Pit was booby trapped. If both the shafts made it to a depth of over 30 metres without flooding, only filling with water when connected to the Money Pit, then it must be only the original Pit that was connected to Mahone Bay. An elaborate protective mechanism had been set by Kidd — or whoever had dug the Pit.

If this were the case, then the men of Truro Company reasoned that there must be some way to block the flood tunnels. Otherwise, how would the original builders of the Pit recover their treasure? If a rabble of pirates could do it, so could the energies of industrious Victorian gentlemen. But first it had to be determined exactly where the tunnels were.

The Truro Company directed its attention to the shores of Oak Island, beginning with Smith's Cove about 160 metres away from the Money Pit. This gently sloping beach seemed a logical place to construct the flood tunnels.

Closer inspection of the beach revealed that all was not what it seemed. It appeared that the larger rocks that dotted the island elsewhere had been cleared away from the cove. More importantly, when the tide receded, water could be seen bubbling up through the sand and stones of the shore. As the water in the Money Pit had already been noted to fluctuate with the tides, it was assumed that this strange flow must be coming from the shaft.

Penetrating into the sand with pick and shovel, the Truro Company quickly determined that the beach of Smith's Cove was in fact man-made. A metre below the sand and gravel surface, the workers discovered a thick layer of brown vegetable matter. It turned out to be coconut fibre. Similar fibres had been found in the Money Pit as well. What on earth was coconut fibre doing there, so far from the tropics — and especially in that quantity? There was literally tons of it. Below this layer was another puzzling layer of eelgrass, a kind of seaweed. This covered a layer of beach stones. Forty-five metres of the shore, from the high to low tide marks, was constructed in this way.

As intriguing as all this was, whoever had built this system would not have placed the entrance of the flood tunnels on the beach, where they could be easily discovered, and where they were only effective at high tide. More digging obviously needed to be done. To access the underwater spot where they assumed the entrance to the flood tunnel was, the men needed to block the advance of the sea. They constructed a cofferdam about 30 metres out into the waters of Mahone Bay. This effectively cleared the floor of the bay, allowing them to continue their search for the tunnels.

Though they didn't find any tunnels, they soon found five drains. These box drains were built from flat beach stones, and had been hammered into place. Converging towards a single point, they angled out into the bay like the fingers of a hand. They met at the beginning of a larger drain. The Halifax newspaper *The Colonist* later described what workers found there: "a number of tiers of stones strengthening the higher part of the drain, on top of which was noticed a coating of the same sort of grass as that already noticed. Over it came a layer of blue sand, such as before had not been seen on the island."

Whenever progress was made in uncovering the mystery of Oak Island, nature — or perhaps some malevolent curse — would step in to thwart the ambitions of treasure seekers. This time a storm blew up which, combined with an unusually high tide, overcame and swept away the cofferdam that protected the excavations made by the Truro Company.

Rather than re-build the cofferdam, which would

have been a difficult and expensive undertaking, the Truro Company decided to build another shaft. This would be the fourth on the island, including the Money Pit itself.

Choosing a spot about 45 metres away from the Money Pit, in line with where the intake was thought to be, the men dug down 23 metres. They encountered no water at all, meaning they had missed the line of the tunnel. Shaft number five was sunk a few metres away from number four. This one reached a depth of 10 metres, at which point they hit a boulder. While the men strained to remove this, water gushed in, indicating they were on the line of the flood tunnel.

To block the tunnel they drove a number of timbers into the floor of the new shaft. That complete, they turned their attentions back to the Money Pit. Bailing and pumping commenced. Workers managed to lower the water level somewhat, but not enough.

Frustrated in every attempt, the Truro Company made one last-ditch effort to beat the Pit. A sixth shaft was dug, slightly south of the Money Pit. This one went down 36 metres without encountering any water, below the point where they believed the flood tunnel connected to the Pit. With luck, the platform of logs at the bottom of the Pit would hold back the water, and the company would be able to reach the treasure from below.

A connecting tunnel was excavated from the shaft, reaching a point directly under the treasure. Even now the mix of water and dirt began to leak around the rapidly constructed joists and beams that supported the tunnel. The men took a break for dinner, gathering their strength for the next and last assault on the Pit. Two workers were left in the tunnel to keep the mud from filling in the shaft. Gammell and McCully were both elated, and a little worried. While they felt sure that the Money Pit was full of gold, they knew that the accounts of the Truro Company were not. This was do or die for them, at least for this summer.

Then came a sound that sent everyone scrambling back to the Pit — a mighty crash, and a rush of water. Running to the edge of the original shaft, they saw that the curse had struck. The Money Pit had collapsed into the tunnel just completed below it, taking all of the tools and 10,000 board-feet of cribbing inside. The new shaft filled with mud. The men working there had barely escaped being buried alive.

Even in the face of death the search had gone on. As one of the workers had run out just ahead of the tide of mud, a barrel-head had dropped at his feet. Although fearing for his life he snatched at it as he passed, and brought it to the surface. Of no value in itself, the only place the barrel-head could have come from was the Money Pit above the tunnel before it caved in.

The elaborate works uncovered at the beach, the tiny chain links, and the barrel-head all added up to treasure. But now that the Pit had once again thwarted the best efforts of the company, would it be possible to convince investors to sink even more money into the Pit?

Chapter 4
The Curse Strikes

The merchant in Chester could not believe his eyes. The man who had come to his store was well-known around the community, a hardworking farmer who lived on Oak Island. By the 1850s, Anthony Graves owned most of the island west of the Money Pit, but he wasn't known to have any part in the treasure hunting. He certainly never claimed to have found anything on his property.

Graves bought his usual supplies — flour, some vegetables from the market, some rum for the cold nights, and nails for fixing up the house. Graves wasn't a chatty sort, he largely kept to himself out on his island. He exchanged some pleasantries with the owner, murmurs about an approaching rain, talk of the latest news from the Legislative Assembly in

Halifax. Then he left, paying for his purchases by leaving a silver coin on the shopkeeper's counter.

The merchant picked it up to put it in his till, but then he noticed something strange. That wasn't Queen Victoria on the coin, nor was the piece the same size as British sterling. And it looked old. The merchant gave a start — it was Spanish! Had Graves found the treasure?

When the Truro Company folded, it took with it the last remaining hopes of John Smith, one of the original discoverers of the Pit, who had been so convinced of the value of the property that he'd purchased several lots on Oak Island. He died in 1853, never having caught a glimpse of the casks of gold he believed lay below his land.

He left his property to his two sons, perhaps hoping that they would find a way to crack the mystery of the Money Pit and make the family rich. It was not to be. They sold their father's land to Henry Stevens, who in turn sold it to Anthony Graves. Graves thus owned the entire island, and he lived there until his death in 1887.

The change in ownership didn't stop the search for the treasure. In 1861, the Oak Island Association was formed. Many of the same partners from the Truro Company bought into the new venture, and they managed to raise $2000 — a very large sum in those days. This time, they would employ the best technology of the day to beat the deviousness of the creator of the Money Pit. Graves gave his permission for the new company to dig on his land in return for one third of all monies recovered.

The Curse Strikes

The area around the Money Pit rapidly took on the character of an army encampment. More than 60 men and over 30 horses were brought over the narrow gap of water that separated the island from the mainland.

Although every previous attempt to bail the Money Pit had been unsuccessful, the Oak Island Association decided to attempt it once more. Clearing away the muck and debris from the cave-in of 1851, pumps were set up to be driven by the horses. But despite having 33 beasts straining away at the machines, the water level in the shaft was lowered only slightly.

Using up much of their remaining money, steam pumps were constructed on the island in 1861. Whatever faith the investors had in this technology was quickly shattered by a sobering disaster, described by E.H. Owen of Lunenburg: "The boiler ... burst, whereupon one man was scalded to death and others injured. The water was pumped out by a large barrel-shaped tube, made of thin materials, and reaching some distance into the pit. The stream of water was conducted from this into the sea by means of a long wooden trough, which extended down to the shore."

This matter-of-fact noting of the island's first death was typical of the approach to salvaging the treasure. Already two cave-ins had nearly caused the deaths of several other men, yet they pressed on, the glint of gold in their eyes. The Oak Island Association was not alone in this — the nameless worker who died in burning agony would not be the last of the dead to haunt Oak Island.

The association persevered and, under the direction of Superintendent George Mitchell, they decided to dig once more in 1862. But now it was not entirely certain where they should dig. It was assumed that the rush of water from the 1851 collapse would have carried the treasure into the tunnel connecting the Money Pit to shaft number six.

Mitchell decided to dig yet another shaft — number 7 — 33 metres into the ground near the Money Pit. This would serve as a pumping shaft, by which means they would empty the Money Pit, clear out the debris, and locate the treasure.

For once, the plan nearly worked. They managed to clear out the water in the original shaft to a depth of 31 metres. However, at that level water began seeping in from the bottom of the Money Pit at a rate faster than the pump could keep up. Mitchell then directed his men to dig a shaft away from the Money Pit in a line to Smith's Cove, in the hopes that they could locate the flood tunnel and block it. Although they dug down 15 metres, and built several branching tunnels from this shaft, they were unable to locate the flood tunnel. Another shaft and more tunnels were dug — the surface and subsurface of Oak Island were beginning to resemble an ant hill — but again, no flood tunnel was located.

Now Mitchell decided to return to the source. If the flood tunnel could not be intercepted before it hit the Money Pit, then perhaps it could be blocked at Smith's Cove. It was theorized that the eelgrass and coconut fibre dug up on the beach in 1850 was meant to act as a giant filter to prevent the clogging of the stone box drains. Running out of money, the Oak Island Association was unable to build a cofferdam that would have blocked the tide from reaching the box drains. Clearing what he could off the beach, Mitchell took what material was available — the clay native to the island — and filled in the five drains.

Again, this method came very close to succeeding. The water flowing into the Money Pit was halved, but their efforts were not enough. The tide came in and washed out all the clay. However, this did finally prove the existence of the flood tunnel. When the clay dissolved the water in the Money Pit became cloudy, indicating that some of the material had flowed into the Pit from the beach.

With single-minded determination, in 1864 Mitchell prepared once more to "flog a dead horse." With the steam pumps, the water in the Pit could be kept down to the 34-metre level. Digging a shaft 30 metres from the Money Pit, the workers built a tunnel that could connect the two. They hoped to intercept the flood tunnel and divert the water to the new shaft. When that didn't work, they dug a number of branch tunnels out from the Money Pit, trying to locate the casks found in 1849 that had been swept away in the collapse.

They didn't find them — but they did find the flood tunnel. One of the Oak Island Association members wrote about it years later: "As we entered the old place of the treasure we cut off the mouth of the 'Pirate Tunnel.' As we opened it, the water hurled around rocks about twice the size of a man's head, with many smaller, and drove the men back for protection."

It took the pumps nine hours to clear the water from this newest onrush. When the workers were able to return, they went in with the company's engineer, Mr. Hill. They discovered that the tunnel had been constructed of round stones, mostly of the type found on the island. "[Hill] put his arm into the hole of the tunnel up to his shoulder ... Nothing could be more particular than our search in the old place of the old treasure."

This newest discovery came too late. The funds of the Oak Island Association were truly exhausted. Death might not stop the efforts of the treasure seekers, but a lack of money would. Although no further mishaps marred the running of their steam pumps, they were not able to keep up with the inflow of water from the flood tunnel, nor determine to where the treasure had been swept. Their grandiose plans in ruins, the Oak Island Association struck camp, loaded their horses and pumps onto their barges, and retired from the field in defeat.

It was becoming clear that however the treasure was meant to be removed, it was not going to be through the Money Pit. The fact that Graves had somehow acquired a Spanish coin on the island without having done any major excavation led some to the conclusion that maybe there was another entrance to the Pit, perhaps one that bypassed the flood tunnels entirely.

It was also beginning to dawn on some of the searchers that the sheer scale of the works on Oak Island could not have been from the labour of pirates. They were disinclined for hard labour almost by definition. Pirates are, after all, thieves, mutineers, and murderers out for easy money. As seafarers lucky to have even a grade school education, they also would have lacked the know-how to build and design the system of tunnels, filters, and shafts that protected the treasure below.

It was only now that attention was finally turned to the mysterious inscription on the stone that had been discovered in the Money Pit 60 years earlier. A conversation piece on John Smith's mantel for years, the stone had been nearly forgotten, a curiosity of little import. But now, with every attempt to defeat the devious engineering of the Money Pit a failure, the men who wanted to liberate the treasure of Oak Island were prepared to examine any clue in hopes of making their fortunes. In 1864, Smith's old fireplace was demolished, and the stone transported to Halifax.

A.O. Creighton, a bookbinder, ended up placing the stone in the window of his business on Upper Water Street. Two years later he had the stone examined by James Lietchi, who was a recently appointed professor of languages at Dalhousie College.

Lietchi looked at the strange assortment of scratches and symbols. He came to a startling conclusion. The message in the stone was in English, and it promised riches just within grasp: "Forty feet below two million pounds are buried."

F	O	R	T	Y		F	E	E	T		B	E	L	O	W
▽	∴	∅	△	✓		▽	∶	∶	△		⊤	∶	⊏	∴	☐

T	W	O		M	I	L	L	I	O	N
△	☐	∴		⨶	∴	⊏	⊏	∴	∴	✕

P	O	U	N	D	S		A	R	E		B	U	R	I	E	D
⊖	∴	﹢	✕	Ⅱ	☉		∙	∅	∶		⊤	﹢	∅	∴	∶	Ⅱ

The stone inscription decoded

Sadly, this is an unlikely interpretation, and was most probably an attempt by Creighton and other treasure seekers to drum up interest in making another attempt on the island. There was no logic in going to the trouble to bury a message just above the treasure. If someone knew where to dig, they would already know what was there. An elaborate code was not needed either, as simply marking the stone with an "X" and remembering what it stood for would be enough.

Genuine or not, the stone remained in the shop on Upper Water Street for several years. It was often used as a beating stone for the leather of the business. Years later, Harry Marshall, who had worked at Creighton's as a boy in the 1890s, described what it looked like: "The stone was about two feet long, 15 inches wide and ten inches thick and weighed 175 pounds. It had two smooth surfaces, with rough sides ... The corners were not squared but somewhat rounded. The block resembled dark Swedish granite, or fine grained porphyry, very hard, and with an olive tinge, and did not resemble any local Nova Scotia stone. While in Mr. Creighton's possession someone had cut the initials 'J.M.' on one corner, but apart from this there was no evidence of any inscription either cut or painted on the stone. It had completely faded out."

No photograph of the stone was ever taken, nor is there a reliable record of the original markings. When the bookbinding business closed in 1919, the stone was given to a local man named Thomas Forhan. After that it seems to have disappeared. Even if it didn't provide answers, it provided what Creighton needed: interest in the optimistically named Oak Island Eldorado Company, of which he was treasurer. The company managed to raise $4000 for the new venture, and operations began on Oak Island in 1866.

Recognizing the need for a different approach, the company decided to take a page from ancient myth. Like King Canute, they would order the tide back. The way to do this was to construct another cofferdam at Smith's Cove, thus blocking the water from reaching the drains that fed the flood tunnel. The company prospectus confidently declared, "There cannot be any doubt that this mode of operation must succeed and will lead to the development of the hidden treasure, so long sought for."

The dam they built was much larger than the one

built by the Truro Company in 1850. The new dam was 4 metres high, and extended in an arc of 115 metres, enclosing the beach at Smith's Cove. The plan was to pump the area enclosed by the dam dry, but once again the effort failed. The beach area was more or less successfully emptied of water, but for naught. Either poor workmanship, or the persistent curse of the island, struck again, and the dam proved ineffective at holding back the sea. It eventually crumbled away in a storm before the Money Pit could be emptied as well.

Again returning to the methods of the Truro Company, the Eldorado group decided to drill in order to locate where the casks could have ended up in the labyrinth of tunnels below. From November 1866 and into the early winter of 1867 they drilled as deep as 48 metres into the ground. They managed to bring up bits of oak, spruce, charcoal, and coconut fibre, but no gold.

Oak Island continued to keep its secrets, but the hunt was not over. The year the Eldorado Company gave up, the same year Canada became a country, a child was born in Thompson Station, Nova Scotia. In 20 years' time he would grow up to dominate the Oak Island search, his passion driving the hunt for six decades.

Chapter 5
The Cave-in Pit

he lot of a farmer's wife is not an easy one, especially in the late 1800s, and most especially when her farm relies on soil as poor as that found on Oak Island. However, Sophia Sellers was a practical woman, and there was work to be done.

On a hot summer's day in 1878, Sophia was guiding the plough behind the couple's oxen, not far from the Money Pit. As much as she dreamed of the wealth that lay beneath her feet, Sophia, like her father, was content to let others do the actual digging. The daughter of Anthony Graves, Sophia married Henry Sellers of Chester Basin. The couple settled on the island where she had grown up.

Still, step after plodding step, she could not help but pay extra attention to the ground as the blade of the plough turned it over. One never knew when some exotic object would be unearthed from the soil of this strange place. Her mind on the ground beneath her and on the dinner she would have to cook when her ploughing was done, Sophia was jerked to the present when the plough suddenly lurched forward and one of her oxen let out a panicked bellow. She was shocked to see that one of the animals had disappeared into the ground. A huge hole had opened up in the earth, swallowing the poor beast whole. The other ox was in danger of being pulled in as well, along with the plough. Freeing the other animal, Sophia rushed back to the farm to get help. The indignant ox was rescued from the hole with some difficulty. The new pit that was left was over four metres deep, and two metres across.

Nothing on Oak Island happened without a reason, and this strange phenomenon was no exception. The Sellers quickly realized that the "Cave-in Pit," as it came to be called, was in a direct line over where the flood tunnel had been assumed to run. Perhaps this was the remains of the construction of the Money's Pit's booby trap.

The Sellers had seen too many fortunes thrown down the Money Pit to become too excited by this latest discovery — children could not be fed on dreams. Life went on as before, but the couple noted the pit, as well as other unexplainable objects found on the island. They had found an ivory boatswain's whistle in 1885, and a visitor reportedly turned up a coin with unfamiliar markings dated 1317!

These discoveries helped fuel the ardour of Frederick Blair, an insurance salesman with a keen interest in the island. Born in 1867, Blair was only in his 20s when he arrived on Oak Island. The young man was not put off by the failures of previous companies. That was the old era. He had been born in the same year as the young and vital country of Canada, which even then was opening up the West and throwing railways across the Rockies.

Blair was determined to go big, and that meant big money. To raise that money, he needed to go south of the border. In August 1892, he opened an office in Boston to sell shares in what would become the Oak Island Treasure Company. The prospectus of the company was written by Blair and Adams Tupper, who had been an investor in all the companies that had dug at Oak Island since the time of the Truro Company in 1850.

The aim of the company was to raise $60,000 by selling shares at $5 apiece. That they were able to do so, despite the failure of every previous attempt on the island, was probably due to Blair's expertise at salesmanship, and the more recent objects that had been found on the island.

"It is perfectly evident," Blair and Tupper confidently proclaimed in the prospectus, "that the great mistake thus far has been in attempting to 'bail out' the ocean through the various pits. The present company plans to use the best modern appliances for cutting off the flow of the water through some point near the shore, before attempting to pump out the water. It believes, from investigation already made, that such an attempt will be completely successful and, if it is, there can be no trouble in pumping out the Money Pit as dry as when the treasure was first placed there."

The company set aside a large portion of its funds to lease the land on the eastern part of Oak Island from the Sellers family. In return, the company gained the right to keep all treasure recovered. Almost every investor that had bought stock in the previous failed companies invested in Blair's venture. Hundreds of others bought stock in the company as well, from all across Nova Scotia and the New England states.

As all of the company's directors were based in Boston, a committee of investors was struck in Nova Scotia to direct operations closer to the island. In the summer of 1894, work on the island commenced once more. Again, an entire compound was created to house the works — barracks for the pick and shovel men, storehouses, an office, and a cookhouse were constructed on the lands not far from where John Smith's old farmhouse stood.

The first job was to investigate the Cave-in Pit in which Sophia Sellers's unfortunate ox had plunged 16 years before. The Sellers had since filled in this hazard to their livestock with boulders from their land. It could be that the Sellers had concluded that the Cave-in Pit was a natural phenomenon, the result of a natural underground cavern. The workers were soon convinced that it was not. Removing the stones, they determined that the pit was circular, with walls hard enough that it was difficult to drive a pick into them.

What was it? The men, including Tupper, a former mining engineer, believed it was an air shaft, built to allow ventilation for whoever had dug the 160-metre-long flood tunnel from the beach to the Money Pit.

Starting from the Cave-in Pit's bottom, the workers excavated the shaft (the 11th on the island since 1795) to a depth of 15 metres. From this depth they drilled down another 5 metres, discovering nothing.

Before any further exploration from there could be made, water broke in from one of the other old shafts. The structure of the pit was considered too unstable to continue, and attention was turned back to the Money Pit.

The men of the Oak Island Treasure Company were not alone in their interest in the Money Pit. By the late 1890s, newspapers were well established as a means of mass communication. Highly competitive for readers, many jumped on the story of Oak Island. And the papers weren't the only ones to capitalize on interest in the new venture. Mahone Bay's nascent tourist industry catered to hundreds of people who were willing to pay for a boat to take them to see the mysterious treasure pit of Captain Kidd.

Ninety-nine years after Daniel McGinnis discovered the old ship's tackle block hanging from the oak tree, the denizens of Oak Island were finally able to make some money from the Money Pit.

"Crowds of people visit Oak Island every day," reported the *Halifax Chronicle* in June of that year. "Every spare room in the half-dozen houses over there has been engaged for the summer. The force is being rapidly increased and ere long General-manager Tupper will have a small army to superintend."

It was now time for the "modern appliances" Blair and Tupper had promised in their prospectus. This was the relatively new technology of dynamite. The plan was to dig a new shaft (number 12) from which a branching tunnel would be dug under the flood tunnel. With a mighty blast, the tunnel would be sealed off, cutting the flow of water into the Money Pit.

Under the eyes of curious tourists, digging commenced on a 17-metre shaft near the supposed line of the flood tunnel. However, with so many shafts and tunnels having been dug and filled in over the years, this proved to be a difficult task. At a depth of 13 metres, water burst into the new shaft from a previous excavation. This was bailed out, only to fill up again with stagnant water, presumably from the Money Pit. Once this was cleared, fresh water flowed in, also presumed to come from the still booby-trapped Money Pit. Finally cleared, the new shaft was lowered the remaining four metres. A tunnel was dug heading out and up towards the line of the flood tunnel, but it was not located.

The large number of shafts that had been dug and refilled over the years now completely defeated the searchers. Henry Sellers and James McGinnis (grandson of Daniel McGinnis) claimed that the Oak Island Eldorado Company had constructed a large wooden platform in the Money Pit just above the water line, before filling the shaft in with earth. However, when Tupper dug into what he believed was the Money Pit, no such platform was uncovered. Had the original location of the pit been lost?

The committee of Nova Scotia investors was becoming disenchanted with the way things were going on the island, and blamed Tupper for wasting time and money. The following year he was removed from his position, and replaced with A.S. Lowden.

Lowden declared that he too would attempt to cut off the flood tunnel, and also "attack the Money Pit direct, nothing having been done there last year." No digging was done in 1895, as Lowden spent the year trying to raise money to buy a steam pump. He failed in this, and he too was replaced by the committee with Captain John William Welling.

By October 1896, the pump had been purchased and work began again. The shaft of the Onslow Company in 1804 was enlarged for pumping. A new shaft, dug near the Cave-in Pit, served as a starting point for another tunnel that was to intercept the flood tunnel, but as it neared the Cave-in Pit it began to flood. At one point the workers were jubilant to enter into a small subterranean tunnel that was supported by timbers. Their hopes were dashed when they realized they had intercepted one of the tunnels dug by the Eldorado Company.

Confusion and frustration reigned, but matters soon got much worse. On March 26, 1897, a worker named Kaiser was sent into a shaft to rescue a cask that had fallen into the depths. Rather than bring up an empty cask, he decided to fill it with the fresh water in the shaft and ride back to the surface on the hoist. This carelessness cost him his life. The hoist broke, and Kaiser tumbled to the bottom of the shaft with the fully loaded cask.

A Halifax paper reported that work then halted entirely — the men had quit en masse: "One of the men had a dream in which the spirit of Captain Kidd appeared and warned him they would all be dead if they continued the search," the newspaper article continued.

Perhaps Kidd had been roused from his ghostly slumber by alarm at the Oak Island Treasure Company's progress. Work did start again after a delay of a few weeks. The men entered the Money Pit, finding the platform that Sellers and McGinnis told them had been left in the 1860s. They also found the Flood Tunnel (also called the Pirate Tunnel), which was the source of all the seawater — and treasure hunting misery — that they had been trying to block all these years. It was a man-made opening with perpendicular sides. In it were beach stones, sand, and a bird bone — all evidence that it connected to Smith's Cove more than 150 metres away.

The ghost of Captain Kidd, or whatever malevolent spirit haunted the island, struck again. Soon after the breakthrough, a valve in the brand-new steam pump broke. The water inflow increased, and the Money Pit yet again filled with water.

So far, Frederick Blair's company had encountered nothing but failure and death. Less determined men would have given up, but Blair and his fellow investors knew from hard experience that Oak Island held more secrets. They would persevere. What they would discover would prove to be the most interesting artifacts yet encountered on the island.

Chapter 6
The Parchment

he worker stepped back from the hole in the ground, trailing a length of cord behind him. He retreated 100 metres, taking cover behind a rise in the ground with a dozen of his colleagues. All around, at a safe distance, workmen, investors, tourists, and residents of the island looked on.

Anticipation was heavy in the air. Suddenly, the murmuring of the crowd was cut short by the blast of a whistle. A few seconds later, the earth shook with a mighty explosion as 160 pounds of dynamite was detonated underground.

Though the blast was expected, the crowd gasped, and some relieved tension in nervous laughter. This was the third such explosion on the island, although the largest attempted by far, as the Oak Island Treasure Company tried to seal the flood tunnel. Within seconds of this blast the workers real-ized that something was different. Where was the plume of water and debris shooting into the sky that had accompanied the other explosions? And what was that bubbling sound?

Some of the men rushed to the edge of the Money Pit, others to the Cave-in Pit. The water in both was in turmoil, boiling and foaming. This could only mean one thing — the two shafts were directly connected.

Workers drilled two more holes to a depth of 25 metres, and blasted loads of dynamite in them. Though the explo-sions sent up spectacular plumes of water, they did not have the dramatic effect of the explosion in hole number three. Although the mighty blast had proved a connection between the two pits, it did not succeed in blocking it, and so the com-pany turned once more to a direct assault on the Money Pit. With the pumps, the water in the Pit was lowered to the 30-metre level and a platform was constructed on which drills could be mounted.

Boring down to 37 metres, the workers once again struck wood — the first time since the tunnel collapse of 1850. It appeared that they had finally found the casks first located by the Truro Company. At 38 metres they hit wood again. Then the drill was brought short, grinding into what sounded to the listeners above to be iron.

This obstacle proved too great for the drill the company was using. A second hole was drilled using an auger, which went as far as 46 metres and then hit cement. Although this could have been a natural phenomenon, further drilling brought up oak chips, coconut husks, and a balled-up material that had an appearance similar to paper. This last item was removed from the island to be examined later. A drill sent down this same hole once again hit what sounded like metal in pieces, but a pipe lowered in the hole was unable to bring any of these up.

A third hole went as far as 50 metres below the surface before solidly hitting iron once more. This proved impossible to bypass or penetrate. Returning the drill to the surface, workers ran a magnet down, which brought up iron filings.

As if all of these discoveries were not enough to indicate the complexity of the Money Pit's defences, one drill hit water at the 38-metre depth. This indicated that there were other unknown passageways underground, possibly another flood tunnel connected to the Money Pit.

The men of the company interpreted the findings of iron and cement as evidence of a chamber, enclosed in concrete and reinforced with iron.

The Oak Island Treasure Company then embarked on a manic program of pit digging. In all, they dug six new shafts, bringing the total on the island to 19. All met the same fate as their predecessors — flooding, collapsing, becoming blocked by boulders, or all three. Often the new work would collapse into tunnels or shafts built by previous companies on the island.

If the men of the company were disheartened, their

activities didn't show it. And it was not all failure. In an attempt to find out if they had managed to block the intake at Smith's Cove, the company filled shaft 18 full of water. The shaft soon drained down to sea level, but no muddy water came out at the beach. Instead, it came out at three different locations on the south side of the island.

The following day the experiment was tried again in the Money Pit. This time, the Pit was filled and red dye added to the water. Once again, the dye showed up not at Smith's Cove, but at the same three locations on the south side of the island.

This went a long way to explaining why all the dams, explosions, and shafts had proven completely ineffective at blocking the inflow of seawater from Mahone Bay. The engineers behind the Money Pit had built in a fail-safe in the form of a second tunnel! The link was conclusively proven when another charge of dynamite was set off on the south shore. As with the earlier charges, the water in the Money Pit became muddy soon after the explosion, as water was forced up the tunnel from the south shore by ongoing pumping in the Money Pit.

Late in 1899, the Oak Island Treasure Company sank what proved to be its last shaft, number 20. Now fully confident that they knew the location of the treasure that had washed away from the Money Pit in 1850, the nature of the chamber in which it rested, and of the flood tunnels protecting it, the men were certain that they would soon have the treasure of the island in their hands. Work was slow due to the influx of water, and it was difficult to get workers. Nonetheless, by April 1900, the newest shaft reached a depth below that of the Smith's Cove flood tunnel.

If the history of Oak Island showed anything, it was that searchers were never so far from the treasure as when they thought they were on the verge of success. This time fate struck in the form of the company's creditors. The members of the company had gone deeply in debt to finance the search on the island. The efforts to find the treasure had begun with a bang, but the Oak Island Treasure Company ended suddenly, its assets sold to fill the deep hole of debt it had dug for itself.

Frederick Blair was not discouraged. Confident that his company had nearly cracked the mystery, he bought out the other shareholders, determined to carry on. Writing in 1898, he said that when the Oak Island Company arrived on the island they knew almost nothing about the nature of the Money Pit. "Our work since has proved that the Pit is not less than 180 feet deep, that there are two tunnels instead of one and that one of them is not less than 160 feet down, and that there is treasure at different points in the Pit ... without a doubt. We have also discovered that the work done by the Halifax Company [the Eldorado Company] is a greater hindrance to procuring the treasure than is the original work."

Confidence and hope undimmed, Blair would continue to try to discover what lay at the bottom of the Pit discovered by Daniel McGinnis more than a century before. But unlike McGinnis, he was no longer certain that the Money Pit concealed the treasure of Captain Kidd.

Three years earlier, on September 6, 1897, the investors and workers of the Oak Island Treasure Company gathered in a room in the Court House of Amherst, Nova Scotia. They were there to discuss what progress had been made thus far, and what would be done in the future.

Sitting at a table, while a few idle gentlemen looked on, Dr. A.E. Porter was examining the various borings and scraps of debris that had been recovered from the drills on Oak Island. Bits of iron and wood passed under his magnifying glass, but there was nothing that excited much attention.

Suddenly, he paused. Here was something different. It was a ball, fibrous in appearance, but not quite like the coconut fibres that had been brought up in the past, nor like the plants native to Oak Island. Dr. Porter peered at it more closely — it was about the size of a grain of rice. With careful manipulation he was able to unroll the ball and spread it out on the table.

It was a parchment — and moreover, there was a tiny fragment of writing on it in black ink. The men gathered around, examining this new mystery under the doctor's glass. What was that scribble? It was only two letters — "ui?" "vi?" "wi?" No one could make it out for sure, and in any case, the fragment only raised more questions than it answered.

Could the parchment be related to the formation of

stones that Captain Welling, foreman of operations, had discovered on the south shore of Oak Island in 1897? The stones formed a triangle, the apex of which pointed due north, directly at the Money Pit. Was this a sign for whoever was supposed to find the treasure?

All this added up to something more than even Kidd's legendary horde. And if it wasn't pirate gold, it was probably even more valuable than all the Oak Island treasure consortiums had imagined. Frederick Blair told the *Toronto Telegram* in 1930 that this was his belief, and the parchment proved it: "That is more convincing evidence of buried treasure than a few doubloons would be. I am satisfied that either a treasure of immense value or priceless historical documents are in a chest at the bottom of the Pit."

Speculation of who built the Money Pit has included every major group that was known to have come to Nova Scotia, and many who were not. Some people have suggested that the Mi'kmaq, who lived in Eastern Canada long before it was settled by Europeans, would have had the time to construct the intricate workings. However, there is no evidence that they would have had the need to hide anything with such an elaborate construction.

Others have suggested the Norse, who made it to North America centuries before Columbus, even building a small settlement in Newfoundland. The Norse theory holds that the settlement at L'anse Aux Meadows was not their only one, and that these hardy explorers also settled in Mahone

Bay, where they lived for hundreds of years. Forced to leave by disease or Indian attacks, they hid their valuables and records on Oak Island. As interesting as this idea may be, there is no evidence whatsoever to indicate there was ever any Norse presence in Mahone Bay, let alone a long-term settlement.

One group that was known to have settled in Nova Scotia for a significant period of time was the French, who founded the colony of Port Royal on the Bay of Fundy in 1605. And it was the French who Franklin Delano Roosevelt was convinced had constructed the Money Pit when he invested in the next effort to recover the treasure of Oak Island.

Chapter 7
Controversy

n the years after 1911, those wandering Oak Island might have been startled to discover a stone, 15 metres from the Money Pit, roughly 45 centimetres high, inscribed with a simple message: "In memory of Captain Kid [*sic*], 1701."

This ironic message, and a host of bad feelings and recriminations, was the legacy of the Old Gold Salvage and Wrecking Company. One of the principal investors in this company was the future president of the United States, Franklin Roosevelt.

Roosevelt had spent much of his youth on Campobello Island, between New Brunswick and Maine. Like many boys before and since, he was enchanted with the pirate tales of Oak Island.

As a lawyer in New York in 1909, Roosevelt had read in the local papers about a brash engineer named Henry Bowdoin. An agreement had been reached with Frederick Blair to make another attempt on the island's secrets. It was Bowdoin who first speculated that the treasure was French in origin. In fact, he believed it was nothing less than the Crown Jewels of Louis XVI and Marie Antoinette. Roosevelt believed this theory as well, although he also thought there may have been other French origins for the treasure.

When Louis XVI and his queen fled Versailles in 1791 during the French Revolution, they took much of their vast royal treasure with them — gold, precious stones, and jewellery of all kinds. However, when the royal couple was captured at Varennes, there were no crown jewels to be found. The story grew that one of Marie Antoinette's ladies-in-waiting had escaped with the treasure. Fleeing the excesses of republican fervour, she caught a ship to Louisbourg, the stone heart of French North America. From there the engineers of the military outpost constructed a safe vault on Oak Island to conceal the jewels.

Romantic as the tale is, it's impossible. The royal jewels were used by Napoleon when he became emperor. As well, Louisbourg had been in British hands for more than three decades before the French Revolution broke out.

Louisbourg does figure into a more sensible explanation for the workings on the island, and one that Roosevelt came to believe in later years. In 1710, the French were forced to give up mainland Nova Scotia, then known as Acadia. They consolidated their strength in the area at their great fortress at Louisbourg on Île Royale, now known as Cape Breton. At the time of its construction in the early 1700s, it was the most formidable military construction in North America, and perhaps in the world. Louis XIV famously commented that he had spent so much money on its construction that he expected to see its ramparts rising above the horizon.

The soldiers, craftsmen, engineers, and civilian officials who lived in and constructed Louisbourg all needed to be paid, and France sent dozens of vessels across the Atlantic loaded with supplies and cash. One of the ships, *Le Chameau*, demonstrated the hazards of transoceanic travel in those days when it sank in a storm.

Perhaps another of these ships had been blown off course in one of the vicious gales that regularly sweeps across the Atlantic and found itself not on Île Royal, but on the English-held mainland. If this were the case, it is entirely possible that the captain of the vessel would not want to risk his precious cargo falling into the hands of the enemy. If he had engineers destined for the fort, they might have been able to construct the Money Pit in the hopes that the treasure could be recovered eventually.

Alas, the records do not bear out this tantalizing theory. The loss of an entire pay ship surely would have been noted, especially by the residents of the fort waiting for their money.

The records don't mention any missing ships other than *Le Chameau.*

If not a pay ship, then perhaps another French expedition can get the credit for the works on Oak Island. Present-day Nova Scotia was a constant battleground between the French and English during the early colonial period, and fortunes changed constantly. Although the Fortress of Louisbourg was almost impossible to penetrate by sea — where the French expected the mighty navies of the British to attack — it was vulnerable from the land. In 1745, American colonists besieged and took the fort.

The French sent a fleet the next year to re-take the fort under Duc D'Anville. Luck was not with the French, and a storm ripped through the squadron. Several ships were lost, the rest straggled into what is now Halifax Harbour (prior to the founding of the British garrison there) and other spots along the mainland. Again, had a stray pay ship from this fleet found itself in enemy territory, they may have thought it prudent to hide their cargo rather than risk capture.

Who built the Pit was of little interest to Henry Bowdoin. Whatever his qualifications for solving the Money Pit mystery, and as a marine engineer and submarine diver he had many, modesty was not one of them. Nor was patience. He showed little regard for the experience of the men who had spent much of their lives working the Money Pit. He told the *New York Herald* in 1909, "Any competent engineer can clear up that work in no time."

Bowdoin claimed he could get the work done in two weeks. At this point, he hadn't even seen the island or the Pit. Nonetheless, in the prospectus for his company he said, "with modern methods of machinery, the recovery of the treasure will be easy, ridiculously easy."

The ghosts of Oak Island do not take kindly to such boasting. Bowdoin and his vaunted modern machinery made less progress than any expedition before it.

"Having hunted treasure in the South with more or less success, enjoying an adventure of any kind and feeling that my engineering ability was equal to the occasion, I took hold of the project," he later wrote.

"With a few more adventurous spirits I formed a company; secured a permit from the Canadian government and left New York August 18, 1909, arriving in Halifax, Nova Scotia August 20. Some machinery was sent from New York, and more purchased in Halifax. We landed on Oak Island August 27."

Arriving on the island in late summer of 1909, Bowdoin found the Money Pit flooded and filled with the cribbing and platforms abandoned by the Oak Island Treasure Company 10 years earlier. He and his men cleared these out and sent a diver into the Pit, in the hopes that it would be possible to locate the treasure this way. Unfortunately, the bottom of the pit was a mess of timbers and cribbing, making this approach impossible.

Using an "orange peel bucket" (a dredging device) they

cleared the Money Pit to a depth of 35 metres and com-menced drilling. Although the drill went down as far as 52 metres, nothing more interesting than cement was found. Bowdoin and his investors, including Roosevelt, were shown around the island by one of the members of the Oak Island Treasure Company. The American had already examined the inscribed stone at the bookbinder's while in Halifax, and wanted to see the other artifacts found on the island. He didn't like what he saw.

Bowdoin saw the remains of the cofferdam built in 1850, but, on examining the beach at Smith's Cove, found no evidence of a drain or an entrance to a tunnel. Contrary to claims that the cofferdam didn't block the tide, he found that it was dry at low water. The ringbolt that was discovered in 1795 was also nowhere to be found.

Despite his skepticism, Bowdoin carried on. He elected to drill at the spot where the parchment had been found more than a decade before. As expected, the drill hit the cement at 45 metres. They drilled through this obstacle, which proved to be 15 centimetres thick. They removed the drill and core sample in order to start clean on the box of gold they believed lay below. They missed it, but at this point Bowdoin still believed he was on the right track, and vowed to try again.

And try they did. This time, they drilled in a grid pattern that they believed would thoroughly explore the subsurface of the island. He put down the holes vertically, and with as wide angles as possible. This way, a large area around the

Pit was perforated to depths of 53 metres. According to him, anything over 60 square centimetres should have been struck using this method. He did find more cement, about 15 centimetres thick, but no treasure.

Bowdoin sent a sample of the cement he excavated to three experts in geology at Columbia University. They all concluded that the "cement" was in fact a natural limestone.

With the operations taking longer than expected, Bowdoin called a halt in November. His agreement with Frederick Blair, who still had the rights to the island, expired soon, and he wrote to him asking for an extension. "I am not satisfied to quit without another try, and knowing now the exact condition, would get to the bottom and clean things up next time," he claimed optimistically.

Blair, however, was cautious. As a shareholder in the Old Gold Salvage and Wrecking Company he wanted to make sure that Bowdoin had the financial means to make another attempt. Bowdoin did not take kindly to Blair's hesitation. He wrote to Blair to say that if he could not get the time extension he would have to give up entirely, and he included a threat: "When finished the Company will want a full report, which one of our people, a newspaper man, will want to publish. The report that I would have to give them would not help in getting further investments in Oak Island."

This about-face did not faze Blair, who wrote back to the American to call his bluff. "Let me say that anything that can be said against Oak Island has already been written, and the publication of any article that you might be able to bring forth would not in the least jar those of us who hold the lease."

War was declared between the two men. Bowdoin's threatened report, as promised, appeared in New York's *Collier's* magazine, in the August 1911 edition. Bowdoin's statements were devastating: "My experiences proved to me that there is not, and never was, a treasure buried at Oak Island. The mystery is solved."

His argument rested largely on the scale of operation required. Bowdoin declared that there was never any need to bury it so deep. The flood tunnel from Smith's Cove would have been 185 metres long, at a depth of 30 metres underground, an unnecessary effort when the South shore of the island would have provided an inlet less than a quarter of that distance. He said that the water in the pit had seeped in through the sand, gravel and limestone that formed the base of the island. He further alleged that the gold watch chain links, the ringbolt, and the characters on the flat stone never existed. He also accused the Oak Island Treasure Company of "salting" the Pit with the parchment in order to spark interest in the company and raise money.

"The sheepskin parchment was not found by the man who did the boring. The borings were sent to the home office of the company, and the first examination showed nothing. A later examination was made, and the sheepskin parchment discovered. (I understand that more stock was sold, and more work done, without result)."

Frederick Blair returned fire in the Amherst *Daily News* early the next year. Bowdoin, he pointed out, was hardly well informed enough to be making any claims one way or the other about the Money Pit. The Yankee engineer had not used any of the experience available to him in the person of Blair or the other men who had spent years working the Money Pit. He had done very little exploration of the site other than his dives and some drilling.

It was highly unlikely, wrote Blair, that the water was seeping into the Pit through the ground, as there were times when water had been known to flow in at a rate of 500 gallons a minute, not to mention it rose and fell with the tide, indicating a more direct connection. Also, the effect of the dynamite near the Cave-in Pit had caused the water in the Money Pit to bubble and churn immediately. While Bowdoin's experts claimed the "cement" was limestone, Blair cited the results of a British company who said that it had been worked by man. He also pointed out that Bowdoin's article had conveniently ignored evidence he could not explain, such as the drains on the beach of Smith's Cove, and the coconut fibres.

To Bowdoin's accusations of faked artifacts such as the rune-stone and the parchment, Blair pointed out that this made the least sense of all. A planted gold coin would have been a more likely ruse than a piece of parchment. Besides, on the discovery of the parchment no public stock offering was made — "nearly all the funds were put up by insiders."

One exception was Dr. A.E. Porter, the man who initially examined the parchment, who was not an investor at the time, but bought into the company soon afterward.

That so many men had invested so much of their time and money — to the point of bankruptcy — was proof enough that the Money Pit was genuine. Why would someone knowingly defraud themselves?

One person who evidently did not buy Bowdoin's arguments was Franklin Roosevelt. He remained interested in the island long after the company he had invested in was dissolved. In fact, references to the island can be found in his personal papers right up to 1939, 30 years later when he was well into his second term as President of the United States.

Chapter 8
Grails and Ghosts

he events that swept the world in the decades after Bowdoin published his accusations in *Collier's* magazine had their effect on Oak Island as well. The Great War, the Depression, and the long battle against the Nazis consumed the energies and the capital of adventurers who might otherwise have tried their luck against the mystery of the Money Pit.

Between 1911 and 1939 no fewer than six companies were formed. Most performed almost no work on the island. Those that did were only able to confirm findings made by previous companies. Frederick Blair was involved in each of them, sometimes as a principal partner, other times as an advisor. As the leading figure in the Oak Island saga, Blair received thousands of letters offering theories, solutions, and assistance in

This photograph, taken in the mid-1970s, shows the area around
the Money Pit. The Heddon shaft, which began construction
in 1937, was 3.6 by 7.3 metres and over 36.5 metres deep.

solving the mystery. Many of the letter writers were crackpots,
but, with failure following upon failure at the Money Pit, Blair
was willing to entertain ideas from any source.

In a 1932 letter to an engineer in New York who was
interested in tackling the Money Pit he wrote, "I have been
connected with it for thirty-eight years, have investigated it
from all angles, and have gathered together a large amount
of data on the subject and I am thoroughly convinced that a
vast treasure lies buried there and that modern engineering
skill and appliances can easily recover it."

One month after writing the letter to the engineer in New York, Blair found himself in the state of Michigan, investigating yet another approach to solving the mystery. The methods were greatly removed from those of modern engineering — rather, they were ancient and occult.

The Michigan visit was a result of a letter Blair received from a John Wicks, who asserted that the treasure and workings on Oak Island were not the work of the Pirate Kidd, nor of the French. He believed that the island hid the lost treasure of Tumbez.

The Incan city of Tumbez in Peru was famed for its wealth. This wealth was greatly desired by Francisco Pizzaro, the Spanish conquistador who visited the city in 1527 and 1528. Pizzaro decided to mount an armed expedition to sack Tumbez and carry away its treasures.

However, he was betrayed by a member of his expedition, a man named Alonzo de Molina. Pizzaro had left Molina in charge while he was away in Spain to get men and material. Molina warned the Incan rulers of the fate that was about to befall them. Acting quickly, the Incas gathered all their gold and jewels, and removed them from the city with Molina's help.

Legend has it that the ships Molina secured to move the treasure were caught in a series of storms and blown far to the north, never to be seen again. And the attempted move didn't help the Incas anyway. Pizarro returned to South America with 250 men, many horses, and some small cannons. With this force he was able to conquer the entire Incan army of 40,000 men. Upon reaching Tumbez and finding it empty of the plunder he sought, he destroyed the city and executed its ruler.

John Wicks believed the treasure had ended up on Oak Island. This answer had been revealed to him through a form of divination called automatic writing. Practitioners would enter into a sort of trance and allow their "subliminal mind" to guide the actions of their hand, which would write the answers to questions on a piece of paper.

In the case of Wicks, he claimed to be guided by spirits "A.R." and "Circle," who had worked on Oak Island centuries before. He was able to describe parts of the geography of the island and Mahone Bay, which he had never seen. Even more strange, some of his writings were transcribed backwards, upside down, and even in Spanish, a language he did not know.

An Incan expedition might account for a number of the strange artifacts on the island. Incas may well have had the engineering skill to construct the Pit, and the inscribed stone could have been left by them, while the parchment could have been left by the Spanish who'd accompanied them. However, to believe that an entire fleet would have found its way so far north, and would have deposited a treasure — much of it sacred objects — without having any hope of recovering it again strains the theory's credibility.

Nevertheless, believing this theory, Thomas Nixon of

Victoria, British Columbia, organized the Canadian Oak Island Treasure Company. During the summer of 1934 the company sent down several drill holes in the vicinity of the Money Pit. They found nothing of any more interest than pink sand, which probably got its colour from the red dye used to determine the course of the second flood tunnel in 1899.

The Incan theory was not the only otherworldly theory that arose in connection with the island. As early as 1897, A.S. Lowden, then general manager of the Oak Island Company, travelled to Boston to meet with a pair of psychics who claimed to be able to communicate with Captain Kidd through "spirit rapping." Other methods used to locate the treasure included divining rods and machines that inventors claimed could locate gold.

The Captain Kidd theory appeared to gain more credence during this period, as well. Gilbert Hedden, a New Jersey automobile dealer, purchased the property that contained the Money Pit after Thomas Nixon's venture failed. At about the same time, *Captain Kidd and his Skeleton Island* was published by Harold Wilkins. The book contained a map that Wilkins claimed had been found in an old chest that had belonged to Kidd. On the map was written "18 W and 7 E on rock/ 30 SW 14 N Tree/ 7 by 8 by 4."

Using this map, which illustrated an island very close in topography to Oak Island, Hedden returned to the stone triangle discovered in 1897. Using it as a starting point, and following the markings on the map, he was able to discover two white granite stones with man-made drill holes. Surveying from these revealed a larger triangle, with the drilled rocks on two corners and the 1897 triangle as its corners. The Cave-in Pit and the Money Pit were along the lines of the sides.

Though Hedden was understandably excited by this discovery, Wilkins, the author of the book, was not exactly a reputable source. He claimed that, though he had seen the map, he had reproduced it largely from memory, making up aspects of it entirely. When told by Hedden that many of its details matched those of Oak Island, which Wilkins had not heard of, Wilkins became very excited. In fact, as Hedden related, "As he became more and more convinced of the truth of my story, Wilkins, and this may be a good commentary on his character and mental capacity, began to be convinced that he was a reincarnation of Kidd or some other pirate and had been selected to disclose the secrets of this long hidden hoard to the world. By the time I left, he was completely certain of it."

Even if Wilkins had basically made up his map, it had given the searchers another approach to use in finding the treasure. If the stone triangle was a clue, perhaps there were other keys to the mystery on the island. The survey approach was to become much more popular in later years. In 1938, however, Hedden was content to stick with the discoveries already made and proceed with digging and pumping as his predecessors had done. He was forced to abandon work when his automobile business — and the IRS, in search of back-taxes — ate up his usable cash.

The soil of Oak Island remained ripe for more theories. As with the Treasure of Tumbez and the French Crown Jewels, any missing treasure of history or legend came to be associated with the Money Pit.

Frederick Blair believed, at one point, that the treasure might have been religious in nature. In the 1600s, when Oliver Cromwell and his Puritan Roundheads ruled England, a large amount of ecclesiastical plate went missing, the result of Puritan distaste for the waste of using gold and riches for gilded crosses, statues, and other church decorations. Possibly these had been removed by opponents of Cromwell to a safer location?

A similar theory has it that the church treasure of the Cathedral of St Andrew's in Scotland went missing after the Battle of Bannockburn in 1314. The Scottish, victorious in that bloody encounter, took their loot from the English to the great church in Scotland. By 1560, searchers there found no gold. The story goes that it had been removed from the cathedral through a series of secret passageways by monks.

One of the most elaborate theories concerning Oak Island speculates that what lies under its soil is the greatest missing treasure of all — the Holy Grail. This theory builds on a number of seemingly unrelated facts, and stretches all the way back to the time of Crusades. It is largely based on a document published in Venice in 1558 called *The Zeno Narrative*, which tells the story of a couple of Italian navigators, the Zeno brothers, who travelled to an island kingdom in the North Sea in the late 1300s. There they met a prince who enlisted their help to lead a voyage across the Atlantic. With a few small ships and roughly 200 men, they made landfall in a strange place with smoking mountains and timid natives. People who studied the document have speculated that the prince referred to was in fact Henry Sinclair, a Scottish nobleman whose ancestral lands included the Orkney Islands. With connections to the Crusades, it is possible Sinclair's family might have come into possession of holy artifacts, such as the Grail.

Frederick Pohl, an American historian, believed that the strange land Prince Henry encountered was in fact Nova Scotia. Using the geographical evidence in the *Narrative*, Pohl determined that Sinclair's landing place was in fact Guysborough, Nova Scotia. According to Pohl, Sinclair travelled from that harbour on the northeast corner of the Nova Scotia mainland to Pictou, in the warm waters of the Northumberland Strait across from Prince Edward Island. As it was getting late in the season, Sinclair sent his men home, keeping only a personal retinue and a couple of small boats.

The *Zeno Narrative* mentions that Sinclair travelled with craftsmen, including masons, who would hardly be needed on a voyage of discovery. However, if he were on a mission to hide something, he might have brought along workers to construct a vault.

Sinclair may have needed to hide something very valuable indeed, if one theory is true. According to one line of supposition, Sinclair was attempting to hide the treasure of the Knights Templar. The Templars were a class of warriors with a special mission from the Pope. Their official mission was to protect pilgrims visiting the recaptured Holy Lands. They were also rumoured to have plundered the Temple of Solomon and stolen the Holy Grail, which could be the chalice used at the Last Supper, the cup that caught Jesus' blood as he hung from the cross, or a mysterious "stone of knowledge." After the Muslim armies evicted the Crusaders from the Holy Lands, the political clout of the Templars declined. In 1307, King Philip IV of France, envious of their wealth, raided all their strongholds in his domain and tortured 200 of the knights for heresy. But the Templar fleet escaped with their treasure, and they were never seen again.

If the Templars sailed north, as some people say, they might have sought refuge in distant Scotland. If they had the Holy Grail, they would have wanted to hide it more securely. They knew Philip was not the only one who was willing to kill for such a treasure.

Once the Templars settled in Scotland, legend has it that they slowly morphed into another mysterious organization — the Freemasons. The Clan Sinclair has always been strongly associated with this group. It is logical that, if the Templars needed someone to perform a risky mission to hide the Grail overseas, they would have turned to Henry Sinclair. He already had a substantial fleet in order to govern the Orkneys. With a Masonic knowledge of engineering, constructing the Money Pit and its flood tunnels would be easy. This theory might also explain the coin, supposedly found on the island in the late 19th century, dated 1317. Although it makes for a great story, the Templar/Sinclair theories are not believed by many.

A more recent tale also ties together some historical conspiracy theories. In this, the treasure of Oak Island is not gold or any other valuable object, but rather manuscripts — specifically the original plays and sonnets of Shakespeare. And why would these need to be hidden? To protect the identity of the true author. Many believe this to be Francis Bacon, an author in his own right and a member of the court of Queen Elizabeth I. As a member of the nobility, it would have been unseemly for Bacon to be indulging in so low a pastime as theatre, especially given the sometimes political nature of his plays. The originals of these manuscripts would have been incriminating to Bacon, threatening his position at court. According to this story, Bacon needed a collaborator to act as a front man for his literary output, and he settled on William Shakespeare, then a young actor.

Later, when the Puritans began their ascendancy in British politics, Bacon may well have feared for the safety of his writings. Bacon had been a member of the Virginia Company, so was somewhat familiar with North America, and had access to men and ships through his friendship with explorers such as Sir Walter Raleigh. It is even possible that the cache on Oak Island may include the fruits of Raleigh's plundering of the Spanish, as well as those of Bacon's pen.

Spanish gold plays a role in yet another theory. During the Seven Years War, the British laid siege to Havana for two months, finally taking the city in 1762. The port was a transit point for Spanish wealth en route to Europe from their mines in South and Central America. Wealthy in its own right, and an important Spanish stronghold, it was a valuable military target for the soldiers of King George III.

When the city finally fell to the British, they were confronted with wealth beyond imagining. Havana was looted of its gold, churches stripped of their treasures, and wealthy families relieved of their heirlooms. There is good reason to believe that some of the gold made it at least as far as Halifax. Much of the money was divvied up between the commanding officers of the land and sea forces of the expedition, and was filtered down through the ranks. Remarkably, there was no provision for a share to the King. This seems highly unlikely given that George III was not well off, and had taken a personal interest in taking Cuba before the expedition sailed.

There is a huge discrepancy between the amount of money that was in Havana at the time (millions of pounds) and the amount the British reported taking (only £737,000). Three ships from this squadron sailed to Nova Scotia bound for the British garrison at Halifax. It is possible that, in an effort to keep the King's share of the gold away from his greedy Parliament, Oak Island was selected as a decent hiding place for the loot. If a warship deposited a number of British soldiers on the island to complete the work, it would have been possible to have kept it hidden, or at least mostly hidden, from the nearby township, which was then only three years old. "Mostly hidden" because one of the persistent legends of the island tells of mysterious men in red coats seen on the island in early days.

Rather than building an underground chamber or series of chambers, it is believed the British put a portion of the treasure on each of the island's 32 lots, which were surveyed years before it became strictly necessary in 1762, when settlers first arrived. The inscribed stone found in 1804, and lost more than a century later, could be the key by which each of the individual hordes could be found.

One more tantalizing theory holds that a failed 1690 siege of Quebec City by New England colonists, led by famed mariner Sir William Phipps, was a decoy. Phipps was known to have plundered Spanish ships earlier in his career. For some reason, he took two months to sail from Massachusetts to Quebec City, although he took only one month to return after the attack failed. Could he have been hiding his wealth?

This is only a brief list of possibilities suggested for the contents of the Money Pit — there are many more, including artifacts left by aliens, and visitors from the Lost City of Atlantis.

Theories spring from the ground of Oak Island far easier than actual gold. After more than 100 years of searching, little had come from the Money Pit but bankruptcy and frustration. The curse that protected the treasure was not to be trifled with. Two had already died there. Soon, there would be many more.

Chapter 9
Death on Oak Island

n April 1, 1951, Frederick Lyndam Blair died at the Victoria General Hospital in Halifax. The heart and soul of the search for treasure on Oak Island for six decades, Blair's death was a turning point in the saga of the Money Pit. For the last 40 years there had continued to be interest in the mystery of the island, but only a few serious attempts had made any headway. Still, none of these had come any closer to conquering the Money Pit. Despite all of these failures, Blair died convinced that there was indeed treasure, and that it could be recovered.

Nine years after Blair's death, Robert Restall moved to Oak Island with his wife, their daughter and two sons. Setting up a tiny home in an old tool shed, the family became a small treasure hunting company of its own.

It was quite a change for the Restalls. Robert and his wife Mildred had performed in circuses all over North America and in Britain in their "Globe of Death." On motorcycles, the couple would zoom around the interior of a large steel mesh sphere, reaching speeds of over 100 kilometres per hour, and passing within inches of each other in the small space. Both Robert and Mildred had been badly injured in these performances.

Perhaps seeking a quieter life, they retired to Hamilton, Ontario, where Restall took a job as a steel worker. However, a visit to the island in 1955 piqued Robert's interest, and he became convinced that he could solve the mystery.

Despite the two deaths that had occurred there already, Oak Island didn't seem to be as risky a venture as the "Globe of Death," although the planning required was just as daunting. The fame — and fortune — that would go to the man who solved the mystery was perhaps reason enough to leave a life of manual labour in Hamilton for the uncertain future that lay ahead in the Money Pit.

Restall did not have the thousands of dollars and heavy equipment at his disposal that many of the previous companies and adventurers did. He sat down and made a detailed study of all of the previous attempts, charts of Mahone Bay, and much of the island itself. He believed that the treasure below was worth $30 million, and by this promise of wealth was able to raise nearly $100,000 from friends and family. With this he was able to buy a large diesel-powered pump from Gilbert Hedden.

Restall believed that the work on Oak Island was not due to any one person or group of people. He believed that it was a pirate bank, "a sort of Fort Knox" built using slave labour and used by any buccaneer with a need to deposit ill-gotten gains securely. There was a precedent for this. The island of Tortuga in the Caribbean had a similar structure — a fortress of tunnels and walls, built using slave labour and used by hundreds of pirates through the 1600s and 1700s.

For five years after moving to Oak Island with his young family, Restall conducted a number of measurements that indicated a mathematical relationship between the Cave-in Pit, the stone triangle, and the Money Pit. Most of the work he did, however, was either by himself, with his eldest son, or with a small team of hired hands. There were no giant crews like the ones that had been sent to the island by the Truro Company and the Oak Island Treasure Company. As a result, the work was long and painstaking, and Restall was not able to make much headway.

At one point, Restall and his older son, Robert Jr., were working on the beach at Smith's Cove dismantling the box drains. His younger son Rick was also there, along with Mildred. One of them, after stepping on a stone, moved it, and noticed that carved into its centre was the year "1704." Many believe that this piece of evidence was a gag played by workers from a previous dig. Nevertheless, it motivated Restall to try even harder to solve the mystery.

Like many before him, Restall believed that closing off the water tunnels at Smith's Cove was the key to breaking into the Pit. He dug a shaft eight metres deep. He was working there on August 17, 1965, with a gas-powered pump chugging away to keep the interior dry, when suddenly he keeled over and collapsed into the pit. His son Robert jumped into the hole to rescue his father, but he, too, collapsed. Four more workmen climbed in, but all were overcome by fumes, including Cyril Hiltz and Karl Graeser. Luckily, Edward White, a fireman from New York who was visiting the island, was able to pull out two of the workmen and bring them back to consciousness with artificial respiration. However, Graeser, Hiltz, and both the Restall men died, victims of carbon monoxide poisoning, probably from the pump.

The curse of the island had now claimed six lives, leaving Mildred Restall a widow with two young children to care for. She had given up much to follow her husband's dream. The family lived without plumbing or electricity when they first moved there. "I have splayed feet because rubber boots were the only shoes I owned," said her younger son, Rick Restall, in an interview with *Rolling Stone* magazine years later. "My Mom went from being a pretty sunny person to a very unhappy one. She became bitter."

She was to lose even more.

If Restall's dig had been comparatively small, the next man to tackle the mystery decided to go big. Very big. Robert Dunfield was a petroleum geologist from California. He described Oak Island as a mere "problem in open-pit mining but with the added difficulty of seeping water."

Where Restall and many of the previous searchers had gone slow and methodical in their approach, Robert Dunfield's approach was to go big, fast, and mechanical. More than any man since Daniel McGinnis found the ship's tackle hanging in the tree in 1795, Dunfield changed the face of Oak Island forever.

Dunfield promised Mildred Restall that he would buy her a house in Chester, but reneged after a few months. He took everything she and Robert had accumulated during their time on the island, including the family photo albums. She continued to live in Nova Scotia until her death in 2004. "My Mom never got over it," said her son, Rick Restall.

Dunfield showed little regard for people, and even less for the clues that might still be found on Oak Island. His strategy of open-pit mining required big machines — a 100-ton "digging clam" capable of moving 800 cubic yards of earth in an hour, and pumping equipment with a capacity of 110,000 gallons of water an hour. To move this machinery to Oak Island he had to build a 200-metre-long earth and stone causeway from the island to the mainland.

With the kind of volume Dunfield was proposing, it would be all too easy to dig up the treasure and not see it in the avalanche of earth being raised by his machines. The plan was to put all the tons of dirt removed from the island through a sluice, which would catch any items of interest.

Dunfield's first line of attack was to scrape the first four metres of soil off the area around the Money Pit using bulldozers. This exposed a number of the old shafts that honeycombed the surface of Oak Island. He then dumped tons of earth onto the beach at Smith's Cove in the hopes of blocking the flood tunnel there.

The next step was to dig a 60-metre-long trench along the south shore of the island. In digging this, he and his workers uncovered a previously unknown shaft that had been filled in, which they excavated. At an 18-metre depth in this new shaft, water rushed in, indicating they had discovered the second flood tunnel. Remarkably, this shaft was due south of the triangle of stones, putting it on the same line of geometry as the Money Pit, the Cave-in Pit, and other artifacts.

Unable to find a branch tunnel from this latest discovery, Dunfield directed his workers to tackle the Money Pit directly. His machines started digging in November 1965, and in a relatively short period of time they had created a crater 45 metres deep and 15 metres in diameter. The effort was costing him $2000 a day, but by late November he was within 15 metres of the treasure chamber.

As had been the case with almost all the other searchers, just as Dunfield believed he was on the cusp of success, fate struck. The owner of the giant crane that was doing most of the digging had to leave the island to fulfill another contract. The replacement crane cracked an engine block. These delays stopped work until Christmas, at which point the workers demanded their holiday time and quit. Over the Yule season much of the sand and earth removed from the pit slid back into the ground. Once work resumed, this backsliding forced Dunfield to re-excavate the Pit three times.

His solution was to make the Pit even bigger, increasing the diameter from 15 to 30 metres across. The shaft would retain this diameter to a depth of 30 metres before narrowing. He ordered the current diggings to be filled in until the winter weather passed, and then he decided to hit the Cave-in Pit with the same approach. He believed that somewhere on the island was an entrance to the treasure chamber of the Money Pit that bypassed the flood tunnels. The Cave-in Pit was the key. Although he succeeded in creating another gaping hole in the ground, nothing came out of the new excavation other than mountains of dirt, stone, and timbers from previous companies' efforts.

Dunfield lost much on Oak Island. The expedition had cost him $131,000. The embarrassing failure, after his confident claims, was a blow to his pride.

The island itself lost more. Even after all his years on the island, it is doubtful that Frederick Blair himself would have been able to recognize the area around the Money Pit. Dunfield's mounds of earth and gaping holes were all that remained. All the careful measurements done by previous companies were rendered useless. The topography of this part of Oak Island was now completely different. The geometric clues in the form of the triangle and drilled stones were also destroyed. The stone triangle slid into the trench when the soil around it eroded. No one knows what other clues were ripped up without ever having been seen.

The people who lived around Mahone Bay were appalled by what had occurred. They recognized that Oak Island was an important tourist attraction, and quite possibly an irreplaceable historical site of national importance. A movement began to lobby the provincial government to purchase the property and turn it into a park, but nothing came of the effort.

Dunfield's attempt on the Money Pit has been likened to making war on the island. War was to come in a different form as the search for the treasure was taken over by two competing groups, with two very different approaches.

Chapter 10
Battle Lines

t the same time that Dunfield and Restall were making their disastrous attempts on the Island, Frederick Nolan was taking a completely different tack. Nolan, a Nova Scotia surveyor, was armed not with pick and shovel, but rather a sextant and map. Nolan's search expanded upon the interesting geometric relation noted by Gilbert Hedden in the 1930s.

Nolan became interested in Oak Island in 1958, after reading a book on the history of the treasure search to that point. He received permission from the owners of the island to conduct a large-scale survey of the entire landform. With the location of the original Money Pit and several of the roughly two dozen other shafts and boreholes lost, this was a long overdue venture. Hundreds of metres of brush were cleared along his grid lines, and concrete markers installed at various points.

The island at this time belonged to Mel Chappell, a Nova Scotia businessman who had led one of the failed ventures in the 1930s. Desperate to make his own shot at the Pit, and rebuffed by Chappell, Nolan went to the Nova Scotia Registrar of deeds to investigate Chappell's claim to the island. He discovered that Chappell did not own all of the lots. So Nolan bought lots 5 and 9 through 14, which made up about a quarter of the area of the small island in the early 1960s.

He was willing to trade his lots for the chance to take a crack at the Money Pit, but Chappell had his eye on other investors. Nolan was left with several acres of land that were nothing but trees, rocks, and swamp. Or so it seemed. With only his own funds at his disposal and no obvious place to begin digging, Nolan turned back to surveying on his portion of the island.

First Nolan decided to attempt to use the landmarks on his property as reference points for new places to dig. There were three stone piles that formed a rough arrowhead, with a base of 30 metres and sides of 45 metres. It was assumed that the piles, which were 1.5 metres high, had been raised to serve as lookouts or guards. Nolan also found two boulders with iron rings set in them. He "drew" lines connecting these boulders to the stone piles, and dug pits where the lines crossed.

He didn't find anything valuable, turning up only an old brass buckle 10 metres below ground. But this in itself was intriguing. It indicated that there might have been diggings away from the complex of tunnels and shafts.

Further surveying yielded even more tantalizing clues as to the work on the island. It also indicated that Nolan's elaborate survey work was not the first such project to take place there. In the course of laying out his lines, Nolan discovered a number of upright sandstone markers, and many of them showed evidence of being placed by man. They were often cut or shaped, with etchings in them, and placed upright, an unnatural position for stones to lie. He also discovered a line of spruce wood stakes, all with rounded tops and buried upright in the soil, only their tops protruding.

In 1971, he dug a pit 200 metres north of the Money Pit, again at the intersection of lines drawn from some of his markers. He found nothing.

"I was exuberant when I started ... I was just like everyone else who's tried to work on the island. I thought I had all the answers but the island has a way of humbling a man," he recalled years later.

His digs were yielding nothing, but the complexity of the artifacts and lines drawn from them were starting to tell him that Oak Island was much more than the Money Pit. The elaborate grid and line system indicated by his finds, he believed, meant that Oak Island hid something much greater than pirate — or any other — treasure. While Nolan was poring over his maps and examining his land, often crawling over it on hands and knees, work continued on the Money Pit.

When Robert Dunfield began his work on the island he brought in a number of partners, including a Florida contractor named Dan Blankenship. When Dunfield left, Blankenship took over. He commuted to Oak Island from Florida for the first few years, then sold his home and moved to the island permanently in 1975.

Digging by Blankenship in the late 1960s uncovered a pair of 300-year-old scissors and a nail, deep underground. Perhaps it was these artifacts that convinced Montreal businessman David Tobias to come onboard.

In 1969, Blankenship became the field director of a company called Triton Alliance. Triton was headed by Tobias, and consisted of a group of wealthy investors from Canada and the U.S., including a member of the Sobey grocery family, a former president of the Toronto Stock Exchange, a Boston real estate developer, and a former weapons designer for the Pentagon. With this backing, Blankenship began an extensive drilling program. Due to Dunfield's levelling of Oak Island's surfaces, all the depths were now about three metres shallower than before. This worked in Triton's favour — it was that much less earth to remove.

Blankenship believed that the intricacy of the system of the Money Pit meant it was possible the treasure was far deeper than anyone had suspected. In fact, he believed that it lay in a vault carved out of the very bedrock of the island, more than 60 metres below the surface.

His drilling program would seem to bear out this theory. China, oak, and bits of cement were all brought up from depths of 50 to 70 metres below the level of the island's surface. Some of this wood was carbon dated to roughly 1575, with a margin of error of 85 years meaning it could have been there as early as 1490.

The drilling program also encountered what appeared to be a number of underground caverns or tunnels, carved out of the bedrock. It is possible that these were natural formations. A few years earlier, construction workers on the nearby shore had uncovered a large underground cavity by accident. However, even if they were natural, it was possible that whoever had built the Money Pit had used one of them as a ready-made treasure vault, and then reinforced it with their own concrete, iron, and wood.

The most interesting shaft excavated by Triton was a hole known as Borehole 10X. About 55 metres from the Money Pit, it proved to be a most unusual spot to drill.

First of all, the drill hit cavities at the 40- and 50-metre depths, and another at 70 metres, more than 15 metres below the bedrock. In addition, small pieces of metal also came up with the drill. In the course of widening the hole from 15 centimetres to just over 30 centimetres in diameter, Blankenship found that Borehole 10X filled up with seawater to the level of the tide fairly quickly. The widening of the hole also uncovered more bits of metal, including wire and chain, not to

Borehole 10X

mention beach detritus, such as bird bones and seashells. This meant that there was likely a direct and clear channel to the sea, probably one of the flood tunnels.

The Triton investors decided to use new technology to explore the subterranean depths of Oak Island, and arranged for an underwater camera hooked up to a closed-circuit TV. The image was blurry. The water was dark and murky, but Dan Blankenship saw amazing objects — a severed hand, wooden chests, and what looked like a body. All of these, left undisturbed in a sealed-off chamber, could have survived the centuries in their tomb without dissolving. Blankenship's snapshots of the television screen were so blurry as to be meaningless to a casual observer. The videotape of the footage was blurry as well, but computer enhancement in the 1990s did reveal what appeared to be chests on the chamber floor. Divers sent into the cavern afterwards were not able to see very much due to the murkiness of the water. Further exploration has turned up nothing so dramatic, nor confirmed the images Blankenship saw that day.

It was Blankenship's belief that the material and photos taken from beneath the island's surface added up to credible evidence that the Spanish had built the Money Pit, using slave labour. The chain brought up could have been used to restrain some unfortunate worker to his station.

The use of the occult to explain the mystery of the island was hardly new, and Blankenship's theory received some unexpected bolstering from that direction in 1973. Dan Henskee, one of Blankenship's workers who had been given a small stake in Triton for his labour, suddenly had a vision. "Dan was in my kitchen when he lost it," Blankenship told a journalist from *Rolling Stone* magazine. "All of a sudden it was like something took him over." Henskee started yelling strange things that made no sense to his friend: "I had to kill you, I had to kill you."

Henskee recalled, "I felt myself being possessed by the spirit of a slave that had been working down there, underground on Oak Island. One of the other slaves had lost a chest in the water, so they chained him to a post. I knew they were going to torture him to death, so I cut his throat, to let him die quickly. I saw it all with perfect clarity, and then I blacked out."

Henskee was sent to a psychiatric ward, where he eventually recovered. However, a few years later he had another breakdown. He fled the island, swimming for shore wearing only a hard hat. He was convinced that the Money Pit hid no treasure, but rather was the very gate of hell. Opening it would bring out the spirits of the damned. Henskee, like many others, still believes that the island is haunted.

Haunted or not, Triton was in the business of treasure hunting. Like its predecessors, the company also built a cofferdam at Smith's Cove, larger and farther out to sea than ever before. It, too, soon succumbed to the sea. Before it did, however, it revealed a number of logs embedded in the sea floor, never seen before. These were arranged in a semicircle. They were notched about every metre and marked with Roman numerals. It was believed that the logs were possibly some kind of slipway or dock. Carbon dating indicated that they were roughly 250 years old.

Another discovery was a stone on the eastern end of the island near the Cave-in Pit carved with the letter "G" in a square. The letter "G" is reputed to be important in Masonic symbology, and many theories about the island involve the Masons.

While the Triton search led by Blankenship made progress underground, and Fred Nolan mapped out the surface of his portion of the island, conflict was brewing between the two. Each felt the other was wasting time with their wildly differing methods. Only one side could solve the mystery and gain the contents of the Money Pit, and as time went on both Nolan and Blankenship invested more of their money and lives into Oak Island. As the years passed, the stakes grew higher for the two men.

Relations had never been friendly between Nolan and the other searchers on the island. Trouble started soon after Dunfield constructed his causeway. Determined to protect his rights to the treasure pit, Dunfield placed an armed guard at the causeway, to prevent anyone from using it without his permission. Dunfield himself would sometimes stand watch there with a rifle: "He was Mr. Macho man," recalled Nolan.

Nolan fought back. He bought a plot on the mainland at the causeway entrance and barricaded it in 1966, preventing it from being used by anyone. When Blankenship took over from Dunfield there was a short truce, and the Floridian paid Nolan for access. Later, when David Tobias became a partner, Nolan acquired shares in the Money Pit and the right to survey.

Sadly, this spirit of cooperation proved to be weak. Once Triton was formed, the agreement between Nolan and the other two men was cancelled. Nolan blocked the mainland end to the causeway again. Triton struck back by building a road around Nolan's property to the causeway, and blocked the other end of it, which prevented Nolan from reaching his own land. He had to take a boat to the north shore of the island to get to his property.

The brinkmanship continued when Nolan chained off an access trail that went through his property. This forced Triton to build another road around his plots to bring equipment to the Money Pit area, but not before Blankenship confronted his rival.

"Dan came out with a rifle and it was rather frightening. The RCMP was called before something terrible happened," recalled Nolan. Blankenship claimed he was protecting his property, but the RCMP confiscated his weapon anyway.

Having come to the edge of a potentially violent conflict, the two sides decided to sit down once more and resolve their differences. In 1971, they came to an agreement whereby Triton received a portion of any treasure recovered on Nolan's property, that both sides would share information of their discoveries, and that Nolan could have land access to his property. In return, Triton wouldn't be able to contest Nolan's property rights.

There the situation would have remained, but for the Nova Scotia Department of Tourism. It was running a sightseeing package to the island, paying Nolan for the right to pass over his land. Then the department widened its access road onto what Nolan said was his property. Again he blocked the road, this time by expanding the Oak Island museum that he operated on the mainland across the thoroughfare. Not inclined to fight, the Department of Tourism turned over its operation to Nolan's rivals.

In 1983, Triton took Nolan to court. The case took four years to resolve. Triton disputed Nolan's right to his seven lots, and alleged he was interfering with their tourism business with his blockades. In the end, the court upheld Nolan's title to his land, but ordered him to remove his museum and other roadblocks. He was also ordered to compensate Triton $15,000. This was reduced to $500 on appeal in 1987. Once the battle in the courts was over, both sides returned to the business of treasure hunting.

Five years later, Fred Nolan approached William Crooker, a surveyor and engineer who was writing a book on Oak Island. Nolan claimed to have made an amazing discovery on the island, saying he'd found the possible key to the whole mystery. Nolan's years of surveying on the island had continued to yield a number of interesting artifacts and correlations between items on his survey grids, but an overall pattern eluded him. That is, until he discovered the headstone.

This boulder, partially buried about 260 metres from the Money Pit, had no special significance until Nolan dug it up with a backhoe. It then became clear that the stone bore a startling resemblance to a human skull. On it was a groove, carved into the shape of a dagger. More interesting still, the stone, once Nolan went back to his maps, formed the meeting point of two perpendicular lines. In other words, it was at the centre of a giant cross. Nolan asked Crooker to verify his measurements. Examining the distances from the cone-shaped stones that formed the ends of the cross, Crooker confirmed that the "almost numerically even ratios of body to arms and top to body suggested to me that what Nolan had found was not an accident of nature."

The cross appears to mark a spot on Nolan's property, as there doesn't seem to be a geometric relation between it and the Money Pit. Today, Nolan believes that it might mark the real spot where the treasure of Oak Island lies, and that the Money Pit is nothing but a decoy. "I may be wrong, but there's one thing for certain. The Money Pit has kept people busy in the same location for two centuries."

And what of the men who were at that location? When the lawsuit against Nolan was over, Triton set about attempting to raise funds for a new, more ambitious try at the Money Pit. The lawsuit had cost the company $100,000. They sent out a prospectus to try and attract new investors early in 1988. The plan called for an enormous sum of money — $10 million. With it, Triton would dig a giant pit, 25 metres across and 65 metres deep. By encompassing almost all the previous shafts dug on the island well into the bedrock, if this plan didn't locate the treasure, then there was nothing to find.

It might have worked, but this time the curse of Oak Island hit Triton — and millions of others — in the form of the October 19, 1987, stock market crash. After such a shock, no investors were willing to throw any more of their cash into the bottomless maw of the Money Pit.

Three years later, the company approached the Atlantic

Canada Opportunities Agency for funding. With a $12 million loan guarantee, the company would be able to employ 50 people and create tourism in the Chester region. The federal economic development agency didn't bite. Nor was the provincial government willing to pony up the cash.

Blankenship and his partners were often at loggerheads as to how to proceed as well. Unlike many of his partners, Blankenship believed the key to the Money Pit was through Borehole 10X. He had dived the hole several times, almost killing himself when the shaft began collapsing in on itself and he was suspended on a cable at a depth of 40 metres. He barely escaped before the steel casing that reinforced the shaft was crushed by the weight of the earth around it, and the walls caved in.

In a sense, Blankenship was now a competitor to his Triton partners. He had purchased several treasure trove licenses (a provincial permit to dig for treasure) in his own name on islands near Oak Island in 1994. Blankenship, and many other individuals, gambled that the builders of the Money Pit might have spread their wealth to several locations. As a result, Blankenship was forced to resign from the board of his syndicate, which now owned a company called the Oak Island Exploration Company, through which they could sell stock.

By then two centuries had passed since Daniel McGinnis had first excitedly shown his pals the clearing with the strange depression in the ground. In that time the island had taken six lives and millions of dollars. It had also swallowed the energies, dreams, and fortunes of otherwise sensible and successful men. With the current treasure hunters bickering and bereft of financial backing, it appeared that the hunt for treasure on Oak Island was over.

Epilogue

From the pleasure boat dock near the Oak Island Inn, Oak Island is just one of many masses of rock and trees dotting the expanse of water enclosed by the shores of Mahone Bay. From the marina it is impossible to see the causeway, roads, and work area that mark the island. The low rise and rocky shore of the land belie the island's remarkable history.

Most summer days the waters of the bay are alive with the yachts and sailboats of residents from New York and Ontario who live in Chester in the warmer weather. Some of the boats are owned outright by millionaires who build summer cottages or mansions on their own private island retreats. Oak Island itself has been immune to this so far. But although it doesn't have famous tenants, it has had quite an effect on nearby communities. Pirate-themed gift shops aimed at the tourist trade do good business in Chester, even if the island has been off-limits to visitors for years.

Early in 2003, a group called the Oak Island Tourism Society was formed. The group wanted to open an interpretation centre and increase public access to the island, which tourists have been not been able to walk on since 1995.

"Oak Island is still one of the top attractions for Nova Scotia," society chairman John Chataway told the *Halifax Herald*. "People have been chasing this mystery for over 200 years. We just want to promote people's knowledge of the island and let them experience it."

There are those in the Chester area who are worried about over-selling the island. One tour operator, who takes paddlers out on the bay around Oak Island, notes that the attraction of the island is in its quiet mystery. Making it more of a tourist attraction could lead to pirate-themed mini-golfs lining the road to the causeway. He fears a "Disney-fication" of the place.

Even if the island itself has been quiet in recent years, it still inspires the imaginations of many, remaining one of the most fascinating enigmas in North America. Books continue to be written about the place, and there are still those who would try to solve its riddle. Even if it never yields any treasure, the history of Oak Island is a valuable commodity for the community and is a heritage site in its own right, although not officially. Many say that the years of abuse the island has suffered should be stopped, and the place preserved for its own merits.

Robert Young, a former industrial designer from Toronto, is one of them. Young managed to convince Fred Nolan to sell him four acres of Oak Island. He visited the area in the early 1990s, and fell in love with the island. His property is marked on either side by what he calls "spite lines" — paths cleared in the forest by Triton to keep Young from setting foot on their property. He's low-key about the work he does on the island, which he describes as more of a conservation effort than a treasure hunt.

"This place is special and it's only original once," he insists. "I'm one of the few people who have actually added something to the island. Some of these guys came in with backhoes and just ripped the place up. If the Smithsonian or some museum would step in, I'd be happy — this was my chance to contribute."

Young's belief of what is under Oak Island's soil is based more on history than speculation. He is well aware of the many theories about holy artifacts or something similar under the soil of the island. "It would be great if it were true, because that would mean there was something here far more valuable than gold. But I don't believe it."

Young has not invested much of his effort into digging. Most of his searching has been limited to "dowsing" (using a stick to find objects, as is done for water), combing the ground with a metal detector, and ground-penetrating radar. So far, he has turned up only buttons and small metal items. He has made two small excavations; one revealed evidence of a well, and the other a fire-pit. This is interesting because his lot was never officially settled. The rest of his time has been dedicated to clearing his land of scrub and dead vegetation.

On Triton Alliance's portion of the island, times are changing as well. To make a concerted effort to solve the mystery will take millions of dollars, and investors are hard to come by for such a speculative venture. It would seem that Dan Blankenship and David Tobias, after about four decades of hunting for treasure on Oak Island, are now willing to pass on the torch. And there are hands outstretched, ready to take it.

In April of 2004, Dan Blankenship did not renew his treasure trove license for the lot he owns on Oak Island. The Oak Island Exploration Company and Fred Nolan renewed theirs, but David Tobias has let it be known that he is ready to get out. He would sell his portion of the island for $7 million to $10 million, but only to the right person.

"My overall interest here is to see the mystery solved and find out what's down there. The very nature of Oak Island attracts strange people. It's an obsession, we're all guilty of it. It attracts a lot of nutty people because its potential, on paper, is of treasures and riches," he told the *Halifax Herald*.

In July of 2003, Tobias approached the government of Nova Scotia again in an effort to get funding for a new dig. He was prepared to lay out the company's entire case for why they believe there is something of historical value buried on their land. He had scientific analysis of the wood and coconut fibre found by their digs, as well as evidence from the Bedford Institute of Oceanography that showed possible manmade structures on the sea floor off the island's shores. His group would be willing to turn over their property to a government or institute for preservation once its historical importance could be verified.

"It's time the island's historic and archeological importance was recognized," he told a Halifax reporter. "Once these people have seen the drilling test, the carbon dating and our scientific reports, they will only be able to conclude the project may be one of the most important projects in North America."

He was rebuffed. The Minister of Natural Resources at the time said that his department was already cooperating with the group by providing geologic information, but that "we certainly have no intention of getting involved in any financial obligations."

Private enterprise may be willing to step in again, in the form of Les MacPhie and John Wonnacott, both engineers. MacPhie has written a book on the island and is vice-president of Geocon, a company owned by the Montreal industrial giant SNC-Lavalin. Wonnacott is vice-president of operations of Black Bull Resources, a mining company. The two have approached Tobias with a proposal that would tackle the Money Pit in a completely new way.

MacPhie and his partner want to dig a number of holes in a circle around the Money Pit with a 30-metre diameter. A system of pipes would pump the holes full of chilled brine. This would freeze the soil, as well as any water coming in through the flood tunnel, right down to the bedrock of the island. Once solidly frozen, the entire area could be excavated with no risk of water flooding the Pit. This new shaft would then be lined with a steel casing.

MacPhie and Wonnacott's plan differs from every previous one in its technical approach, and also in their intention to not only solve the mystery, but to make the fruits of their labour available to the public. The soil removed would be carefully screened for any artifacts of note, which would then be placed in a museum. The museum would be built underground, in the Money Pit itself. This would include a full-scale replica of the treasure chamber, for which they believe the Money Pit is an access point.

The pair has already been in contact with Tobias, but they need $15 million to make their plan work. Will a new approach be enticement enough to attract new investors? Tobias is ready to let them try. After so many years, it is time for him to enjoy his time with his wife. As he told the *Halifax Herald* in 2004, "I think she's tired of it. She thinks it's about time I wrapped it up."

MacPhie and Wonnacott are confident that with modern technology and careful study, they will succeed where so many have failed.

"There is no doubt that excavation of a deep shaft, in conjunction with appropriate historical and archeological studies of recovered items and exposed workings, would finally resolve the Oak Island mystery," they wrote in a report on their plan.

People still share stories and legends about Oak Island. Some say the treasure will never be found until the last oak is gone. Others say it won't be found until a seventh person dies in search of it. Others think some magic is needed to lift the curse. Will new technology ever solve the mystery? Only the

Epilogue

old ghosts that haunt the quiet island can know for sure. For now, the Money Pit yields only more questions.

Further Reading

Crooker, William. *Oak Island Gold*. Nimbus, 1993.

Finnan, Mark. *Oak Island Secrets: The Treasure and the Treasure Hunters*. Formac Publishing, 1995.

Harris, R.V. *The Oak Island Mystery*. McGraw-Hill Ryerson, 1958.

MacPhie, Les and Harris, Graham. *Oak Island and Its Lost Treasure*. Formac Publishing, 1999.

O'Connor, D'Arcy. *The Big Dig*. Ballantine Books, 1988.

Acknowledgements

Direct quotes in this book come from many different sources. Much of my material on Robert Restall and his family was derived from an excellent article in the January 22, 2004, *Rolling Stone Magazine* article by Randall Sullivan, "The Curse of Oak Island." R.V. Harris' volume *The Oak Island Mystery* remains one of the most thorough books on the topic. William Crooker's *Oak Island Gold* is an excellent resource and benefits from his association with Fred Nolan.

I would like to acknowledge Les MacPhie, whose book, *Oak Island and its Lost Treasure,* brings a scientific rigour to the engineering problems behind the original diggings on the island and how the mystery might be solved.

Both my parents, Sharon and Paul Reynolds, were diligent in clipping newspaper articles on Oak Island from the *Halifax Herald,* which I relied on for much of the epilogue, and also must be thanked for introducing me to the Holy Grail connection to my home province.

I am indebted to Gord Tate of Mahone Bay Kayaks, who escorted me to Oak Island and introduced me to Robert Young. Robert was kind enough to share with me his insights on the mystery, and his part in the custodial efforts on this mysterious chunk of land. They spoke to me for an article I wrote for *explore* magazine, to whom I am also grateful for my first opportunity to write on this subject. Also, I am grateful for the assistance of the Nova Scotia Department of Tourism.

Most especially, I would like to extend a heartfelt thanks to Jill Foran and Kara Turner at Altitude Publishing, and my editor Laurie Wark, all of who helped me turn my "Hey, Pirates! Cool!" excitement into what I hope is an interesting and informative book.

About the Author

Originally from Nova Scotia, Mark Reynolds is a Montreal writer and editor.

Photo Credits

Cover: Government of Nova Scotia; Danny Hennigar, Oak Island Tourism Society: pages 21, 79, 104.

Amazing Author
Question and Answer

What was your inspiration for writing about Oak Island?

I grew up in Nova Scotia, and had read about the island when I was 10 years old, in an adventure book called *The Hand of Robin Squires*, by Joan Clark. The idea of buried treasure and a curse struck my imagination, and stayed with me ever since.

What surprised you most while you were researching the topic?

I was most surprised by the amount of money — and the number of human lives — that had been lost in pursuit of the treasure. It's sad to think of what people are willing to risk for greed and glory.

What do you most admire about the people you researched?

I'm most impressed by the determination and ingenuity that so many have shown in trying to beat the mysteries of the Money Pit.

Which of the escapades featured in the book do you most identify with?

I remember when I was a kid playing with my friends, exploring the woods near our houses and digging in holes or under trees we thought looked interesting. I guess we hoped we would be able to be like Daniel McGinnis when he found the Money Pit back in 1795.

What difficulties did you run into when conducting your research?

Fortunately, there's a lot of good material out there on Oak Island — there have been many newspaper and magazine articles over the years. What is more difficult is getting information from the current owners. Even those who were happy to help me don't want to reveal too much information regarding their future plans; everybody wants to be first to solve the mystery!

Why did you become a writer? Who inspired you?

I became a writer because I love telling stories, and I especially love telling stories about Canada's history. Growing up, I was a big fan of Farley Mowat, and I hope I can have half the career he has! My teacher in Grade 5, Mr. MacKinnon, was always very encouraging of my reading (even when I would read in class!), while my older sister was always a very good writer, and would compose stories for me and my younger sister. I remember that I wanted to be able to entertain people like that, too. And of course my parents both encouraged and supported me to write as well, even if they secretly thought it was crazy!

Who are your Canadian heroes?

Anyone who takes a risk or makes a sacrifice to do what they know is right. One man I'm impressed with is Lt. General Romeo Dallaire, who has dedicated his life to preventing another tragedy like the Rwanda genocide from happening again.

Which other Amazing Stories would you recommend?

There are so many, but I'll pick *The Mad Trapper* by Hélèna Katz.

Amazing Places to Visit

The Maritime Museum of the Atlantic in Halifax has displays of shipwrecks and privateering, and includes gold coins salvaged from sunken vessels.

The Settler's Museum in Mahone Bay shows what life was like in the early days in the settlements around Oak Island. Oak Island itself can be easily seen from the wharf in town.

Campobello Island, where Franklin Roosevelt grew up, is the site of a museum and international park. It is in the Bay of Fundy, not far from St. Stephen's, New Brunswick.

Index

Index